BRITISH FOLK ART

British
Folk
Art

James
Ayres

THE OVERLOOK PRESS
Woodstock, New York

© 1977 Carter Nash Cameron Limited

First published in the United States in 1977 by
The Overlook Press, Lewis Hollow Road, Woodstock,
New York 12498

ISBN 0–87951–060–9

Library of Congress Catalog Card Number: 76–57876

Produced by Carter Nash Cameron Limited,
25 Lloyd Baker Street, London WC1X 9AT

Designed by Tom Carter
Picture research by Philippa Lewis
Edited by Carolyn Eardley

Set by Trade Linotype Limited, Railway Terrace, Nechells,
Birmingham B7 5NG.
Printed by Page Bros (Norwich) Limited,
Mile Cross Lane, Norwich NOR 45N.
Bound by Dorstel Press Limited, Edinburgh Way, Templefields,
Harlow, Essex.

Printed and bound in Great Britain.

Illustration on back of jacket: A painted folding table from a canal
boat.

Contents

Foreword

Folk art is much more highly regarded and eagerly sought after in America than is its equivalent here in Britain. Here both natives and visitors are more concerned with the great country house and its contents, and the indigenous culture of the ordinary people has until lately been largely disregarded. As recently as 1938 it was possible for an article in a learned journal to dismiss folk art as being 'mostly of an uncultured nature'.[1]

The Second World War, however, did something towards changing our values. We super-taxed our aristocracy and developed a new interest in the democratic arts. The Lion and Unicorn Pavilion at the 1951 Festival of Britain was not an answer to this interest, but was symptomatic of it. It was a 'welcome home' for the returning serviceman, a celebration of Englishness after austerity.

This interest in British popular art was also expressed in book form at this time, for example Barbara Jones' *The Unsophisticated Arts* (Architectural Press 1951) and most notably *English Popular Art* by Enid Marx and Margaret Lambert (Batsford 1951). Later, in 1958, Marx and Lambert organised and exhibition of popular art at the Museum of English Rural Life at Reading. In the introduction to their catalogue they wrote:

> The term 'popular art', though we may none of us find it entirely satisfactory . . . has the merit of being sufficiently elastic to include not only handicrafts and things made, either by professionals or amateurs in the country-side itself but also such things made to country needs and tastes, in towns and by machinery, or even imported from abroad.

English 'folk art' on the other hand is not so diverse; although it may be found in town or country, it does not include imported or mass-produced items. Ultimately the definition must be subjective, as must the application of those outrageous generalisations, 'fine art' and 'applied art'.

In general this book follows the example set by students of American folk art and in particular the book and exhibition *The Flowering of American Folk Art 1776—1876* by Jean Lipman and Alice Winchester.

> Since no two specialists in Europe and America can agree on exactly what folk art is, the authors simply made their selection outside the territories held by the scholars and collectors of fine arts and academic artists.[2]

Although numerous exhibitions and books have appeared on American folk art* it is remarkable that the equivalent work in Britain has been virtually ignored. I hope, in this book, to correct that situation. At a time when the democratic spirit has made us more concerned with the history of the ruled rather than their rulers, surely our enthusiasm for the art of the people is likely to be more real than are our sensibilities towards the art that was patronised by an outmoded élite or an out-dated theology.

This work is a dithyramb in honour of folk art, and I make no apology for my own enthusiasm for the work of these often anonymous artists. Above all folk art was an activity. It was not developed out of intellectual theory, neither was it limited by it: its discipline was craftsmanship. Today we view this work as the product of a Garden of Eden before The Fall.

*The first exhibition of American folk art was held in 1924 at the Whitney Studio Club (now the Whitney Museum of American Art), New York City.

REFERENCES
1 *Archaeological Journal*, vol. XCV, 1938, part 1. 'Mural Decoration' by Francis W. Reader.
2 Review in *Antiques* magazine (USA), June 1974.

Introduction

Promiscuous though the Victorians may have been in their aesthetics, the potency of their successive beliefs and their prolific expression today command considerable respect. 'The establishment' had the genius to pick Joseph Paxton's Crystal Palace and the confidence and arrogance to ignore that with which they were not amused. Theirs was the truly permissive society. They permitted other values (as well as vices) to survive. Now that we are given Design by Centres, Craft by Councils and Patronage by Committees, we suffer a monstrous uniformity. In spite of industrialisation, and sometimes because of it, the Victorian period produced many fine works of folk art. Ship and roundabout carving, together with scrimshaw, reached a height of perfection in the nineteenth century in both Britain and America. On the other hand, shop, trade and inn signs were at their best in the first half of the eighteenth century, after which bylaws discouraged their use in Britain.

Folk art is uncommon in England perhaps because, in a sense, the whole of the British Isles was metropolitan and therefore non-provincial. The wealth generated by the exploitation of the Empire financed a cultural superiority. Although 'high art' remained the concern of a small élite, its influence permeated almost everywhere. Furthermore, the British Isles are small and the great landowners visited their estates regularly. This had the effect of keeping even Scotland and Ireland at least in annual contact with the latest fashions from London. As a result, Britain can boast little folk furniture that would not better be described as provincial. For those who had pretensions to polite society, portraiture was a necessary concomitant, but only in such portraits as could themselves be described as 'polite'. Consequently a great many provincial portrait painters achieved metropolitan standards. In fact, many of the great names in eighteenth-century English portraiture began their careers in the provinces.

'Folk art' is a term which, being wide in scope, includes the work of professional craftsmen of great artistic ability which nevertheless falls outside the conventions of fine-art. In the small-scale, self-sufficient economy of the village, many of the inhabitants would have derived their livelihood from more than one skill, and I have known a number of skilled stone masons even in today's England who have also been small farmers. The amateurs, the non-professionals, were often women who used their skill with the needle to make all manner of 'pictures'. In addition, they applied dexterity and artistry to making two-dimensional and relief objects by sticking together shells, straw, cloth and seeds. Although such confections may sound grotesque, and could be described as the occupational therapy of a too leisured class and sex, they can be seen today by us, who are remote from the conditions that produced them, as works of art, as also can the watercolours by army officers in the Crimea, the pictorial records by sailors of their voyages, and a fretwork steam-engine complete with fretwork steam! Many of these objects fall within the purview of this book as folk art, no matter that some of the 'folk' were from elevated stations in life.

Fretwork model steamroller made by F. JENKINS, ENGINEER, OXFORD c1900. 24in x 18in.

Although some areas are clearly central to the study of folk art, its limits are less clear. Art knows no frontiers. 'Folk art' remains a term with which we must live, and it is surely better than the many alternatives. 'Naive art' as a term implies a total lack of sophistication but, more often than not, the folk artist exhibits a technical mastery over the handling of materials that often exceeds the performance of the so-called 'academic' artist (in, for example, the disastrous use of bitumen by Sir Joshua Reynolds). Sometimes, too, this allegedly 'naive' work reveals truer drawing than that of the patrician contemporary which was often distorted by the imposition of the conventions of fashion ('classical' proportions for the human body were often ludicrously remote from reality). 'Peasant art' surely refers to that which grew out of an exclusively agrarian background in post-medieval but preindustrial Europe. 'Popular art' always exists where popular views are possible or permitted, and embraces many subjects. Barbara Jones in her book *The Unsophisticated Arts* looks not only at the 'Demountable Baroque' of the fair-ground but also at the 'dags' of the railway station, the dragons of the tattooing 'professor' and the automata of the pier, together with ice-cream cones, sweets, pies and bread. Delicious though many of these subjects are, they tend towards a rather indigestible conglomerate. This book is mainly concerned with what might be loosely termed the 'sculptural' and the 'pictorial'. I have included a number of examples that border regions of sophistication, and numerous utilitarian articles that were made with great artistry and which exceed the requirements of necessity. I have excluded objects that were mass produced, and the products of the printing press are similarly disregarded except where, as for example in the case of trade labels, they help to throw light on folk art.

All art is a part of the ethnology of man but I have omitted those objects, the late survivals of ancient, tribal and pre-

Left: a hippah *(village) in New Zealand, painted by an unidentified seaman on one of Captain James Cook's voyages of discovery. 6in x 5½in. This was the ultimate source for the engraving which appeared in the published account of the voyages, here* (above) *shown in reverse.*

Roman Britain, which were made for festivals that died out in the early nineteenth century or which have survived as a pale imitation. Easter eggs in Britain today bear little resemblance to those described by Howitt in the nineteenth century:[1]

> Pace-Eggs [Pasque] . . . which are almost as ancient as the Ark . . . seem now to have retired northward in England . . . They are boiled hard and beautifully coloured . . . some by boiling them with different coloured ribbons bound round them, others by colouring them of one colour, and scraping it away in a variety of figures; others by boiling them within the coating of an onion, which imparts to them the admired dye.

In some villages Washington Irving saw (as described in his *Sketch-Book*) gloves and garlands of cut paper hung up in the churches at the funeral of a maiden. Howitt, although he never witnessed such a funeral, remembered 'seeing those gloves and garlands hanging in my native village in Derbyshire; and I have heard my mother say . . . she has helped cut and prepare them'. Apparently the cut paper versions were the successors of actual flowers and real kid gloves. The custom persists in Abbotts Ann in Hampshire.[2]

When the harvest was safely gathered in, corn dollies were made from the last stook in the last field. Frazer in *The Golden Bough* associates this practice with the worship of the goddess Demeter in ancient Greece. The forms of these 'dollies' have regional associations in Britain and they were customarily hung in the main room of farmhouses and

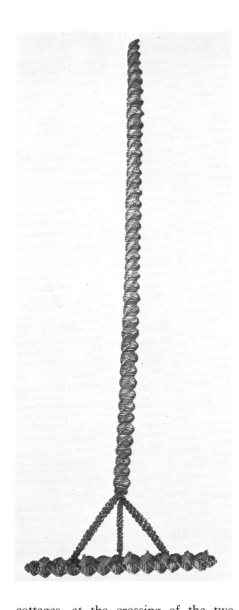

Corn dollies from the Museum of English Rural Life at the University of Reading. Right: a farm worker making a corn dolly.

cottages, at the crossing of the two main beams of the ceiling,[3] to be renewed when the next year's harvest brought forth a new 'crop' of dollies.* Such manifestations of Britain's tribal customs abound: the Mari Lwyd of Wales, the Lair Bhan of Ireland and the Isle of Man, the Wren Houses decorated with coloured ribbons in Pembrokeshire,[3] the Cross-Dressing of Ilkeston, and the Well-Dressing of Tissington, all are surviving or only recently extinct examples of a culture so primitive and distant that their meaning has been forgotten or corrupted in the service of Christianity.

In medieval times art was the province of her practition-

*The Horniman Museum in London exhibits corn dollies drawn from all over Europe.

ers who placed it at the service of prince or prelate. As the Renaissance took its foreign grip on northern Europe, the theorists took command. Architects gained ascendancy over masons and some artists were even able to dominate their clients—'our present Sculptors of eminence will not submit to the directions of the *ignorant* employer'.[4] The founding of academies in the late eighteenth and early nineteenth centuries simply ossified a trend that was at least two hundred years old. The visual folk arts are those that, for one reason or another—usually a happy sort of neglect—

were not subjected to the class system, which resulted in an ever widening gulf between the designer and the maker. As the high culture moved on, a variety of areas of visual expression managed to preserve the vitality born of an identity of inspiration and execution. Designs could evolve as they were made, for the designer and the maker were one and the same. Objects made in this way are many and various, among them inn and trade signs, nineteenth-century ships' figureheads, and toys. Folk painters similarly worked at their craft and made their own pigments and frames. They ignored the more philosophical characteristics of the 'fashionable' painter as epitomised by Reynolds in his *Discourses to the Royal Academy Schools*. Even those amateur painters who were persons of fashion often produced watercolours and embroideries in which the lack of technique, in craft or draughtsmanship, has produced an object that disregards the 'fashionable' precepts with which its maker was familiar.

The aristocratic world of the seventeenth, eighteenth and nineteenth centuries in general took art to be architecture, sculpture and painting. Sculptors were concerned with marble and painters were concerned with oil paint. The folk artist did not have such a limited outlook and many materials, old and new, were used; some of these are described in Chapter 1.

Folk art is the art of a sub-group, often in the majority but not representing the dominant culture. It does not to my mind make its appearance in England until serfdom died out and money became available to a wider class of people. Industrialisation did not arrest the growth of folk art. The painted roses and castles of the narrow boat, for example, did not appear until the canals were in decline after 1830. Although the development of steam-powered ships and the iron hull resulted in a decline in ship carving, it was steam power that also drove the large fairground roundabouts which bore such a weight of carving often made by ex-ship carvers. Industrialisation, then, does not account for the demise of folk art. Rather this was the result of the emergence of technology. The years between approximately 1603 and 1914 are accordingly the period with which this book is mostly concerned.

The authority of the monarchy over things temporal and the church over things spiritual united most of medieval Europe in one culture. The modern world, democratic though it may sometimes be politically, is enthralled by its own technology, and its communications are so effective that a single culture is inevitably emerging once again. Just as the old national characteristics are blurring because of our technology, so technology has absorbed just those abilities that once found expression in the old crafts. It is not that

Chelsea Old Church, *oil on card, late 19th century, attributed to Walter and Henry Greaves, two Thames boatmen who were befriended by the painter J. M. Whistler.*

craftsmanship is dead, rather that it has found new outlets. With the old vision and the old crafts gone or going, so folk art is a thing of the past and those who would maintain the fabric of our physical heritage will perforce, and quite apart from the sentiments of a scientific age, speak of conservation rather than restoration.

It was over a century before Hogarth's interest in the standards of another cultural level, namely signboard art, was repeated. The French Impressionists adopted the douanier Rousseau, and Whistler the Greaves brothers; in our own century, Ben Nicholson promoted the work of Alfred Wallis. That such a trend has often been the kiss of death to such artists is unimportant: what is important is the trend itself. The Victorian antiquary dismissed the art of many continents by cataloguing such work under that dangerous word 'ethnography'. In this respect it has taken the intuitive flair of the artist to assist the intellectual judgement of the scholar.

1   William Howitt, *Rural Life of England*, 1840.
2   Margaret Lambert and Enid Marx, *English Popular Art*, London, 1951.
3   See Iorwerth C. Peate, *Tradition and Folk Life—a Welsh View*, Faber, London, 1972, illus. 50, 45, 46, 47.
4   J. T. Smith, *Nollekens and his Times* (1828), new ed. 1919.

Methods
and Materials

Art historians, quite properly, are concerned with the significance of content and form and with aesthetic innovation and tradition. Material considerations are often forgotten, however, and are ignored at great risk. The vegetable or mineral used in the creation of an object always influences and sometimes dictates its character. Equally significant is the means by which these substances are controlled and made into objects of various sorts. In the consideration of 'folk art' these are especially important factors, and it is essential to abandon some of the prejudices and to ignore much of the snobbery implicit in so much 'high art' criticism.

The visual arts have long been dominated by painting, and the art historian is too often in fact a biographer of painters, rather than an historian of paintings. Folk art as a relatively new area of study is refreshingly free of such inhibitions and limitations; oil painting is but a part of a much more important whole.

Folk art may be divided into two: the work of the unsophisticated craftsman with sophisticated techniques; and the work of the aristocratic dabbler with an urbane condescension towards a tasteful watercolour. The former for the most part relied upon tradition, upon the word of mouth of the master who had trained him in the 'art and mystery' of his craft. It was the amateur who was in most need of the instruction manual. Ultimately, such manuals were widely used by 'professional' and 'non-professional' alike, but the earliest of these was addressed to the 'profit of anyone who wants to enter this profession'. This book, the fifteenth-century Il Libro dell' Arte by Cennino d'Andrea Cennini[1], is concerned primarily with painting, but also includes descriptions of for example, 'How to Cast Medals.' Although Cennini emphasises that an aspiring artist should possess 'Enthusiasm, Reverance, Obedience, and Constancy', and that 'The basis of the profession, the very beginning of all these manual operations is drawing and painting', he orders a thorough knowledge of the following:

> . . . how to work up or grind, how to apply size, to put on cloth, to gesso, to scrape the gessos and smooth them down, to model with gesso, to lay bole, to gild, to burnish, to temper, to lay in; to pumice, to scrape

through, to stamp or punch; to mark out, to paint, to embellish, and to varnish, on panel or ancona.

Painting itself was therefore only one of a whole series of crafts that the Renaissance painter was expected to master. The introduction of tube paints in the mid-nineteenth century was an innovation that divorced the painter from a direct understanding of his materials and today painting may no longer be regarded as a craft. Harold Osborne in the Oxford Companion to Art,[2] argues that Cennini's book 'stands between the medieval and the modern periods in content and outlook . . . preserves the medieval precepts and technical formulae [and is] modern in its insistence on innovation.' The mysterious Theophilus (probably a German monk and craftsman in metal) was, in his De Diversis Artibus, deeply concerned with methods and materials, but he does also give some impression of the medieval artist's outlook. His book has been dated by his translator and editor, C. R. Dodwell,[3] to between 1110 and 1140.

It was on this medieval basis that the craft guilds of England functioned, and as with Theophilus and Cennini* religion played a significant part in the life of guild members. By the fifteenth century and more often in the sixteenth and seventeenth centuries the guilds in England, whose jurisdiction was confined to the towns in which they were located, tended to amalgamate, and in some towns all the craft guilds were merged into a single fraternity. They managed to preserve their independence from the state, but the Tudors maintained a policy designed to bring them under national control. In 1503 laws were passed requiring 'fellowships of crafts or mysteries' to be approved and registered by the Royal Justices or other Crown officers. The statute of 5 Elizabeth c.4 also curtailed their jurisdiction over journeymen and apprentices. Their remaining privileges were not formally abolished until 1835. (It is interesting to note that William Morris was born in 1834.)

The guilds were not designed simply to uphold a monopoly and the income of their members; they were also concerned with conditions and hours of work. But above

*'Here Begins the Craftsman's Handbook, made and composed by Cennino of Colle, in the reverence of God, and of the Virgin Mary, . . .'

all, they maintained the quality of the craft that they fostered and represented. After the formal abolition of their privileges in 1835, traditional craftsmanship began its decline. This situation was confirmed by the new skills of industrialisation which were by this time 'of an age' to take over.

Once the craft guilds had lost ground during Tudor times their monopoly was no longer secure, and by the seventeenth century manuals on various crafts began to appear. The 'art' remained; the 'mystery' was gone. I quote liberally from these manuals, for in them may be heard the authentic voice of the craftsman and, by extension, of the folk artist, many of whom must have found such books invaluable. The authors often display an understanding of the use of materials that can only be explained by direct experience:

> Lay on your gold . . . if your work be sufficiently moist, you'll perceive how lovingly the gold will embrace it, hugging and clinging to it like those inseparable friends, Iron and Loadstone.[1]

Surprisingly, many of these very early manuals were directed not only at artists but also at the élite, the leisured classes. John White published *A Rich Cabinet with a Variety of Inventions*, 'Unlock'd and opened, for the recreation of Ingenious Spirits at their vacant hours', in London in 1651.

The contents of this book are, to say the least, diverse, a fact which White excuses in his preface by pointing out that 'the laborious Bee gathereth her cordiall Honey, and the venemous Spider her corroding poyson many times from one Flower'. The book contains a series of short instructions on various subjects, including those associated with the visual arts:

6) To have pretty sport at Cock-fighting with a single Cock.

39) How to refresh old Pictures and make them look as if they were new.

44) A pretty way how to cast flowers in Wax of divers colours.

45) How to make a bunch of Grapes in Wax, which will seem natural.

47) How to Inlay Boxes, Cabinets, or the like with hard Wax.

59) An excellent way of baking Bread without a hard crust.

Left: *A page from John White's* A Rich Cabinet with a Variety of Inventions *(1651)*. Centre and right: *Frontispiece and title page of William Salmon's* Polygraphice or The Arts of Drawing Limning Painting &c *(1701)*.

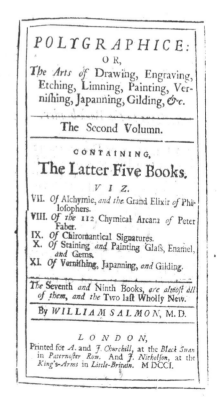

60) A dainty glistening plastering for Seelings, or
for Walls.

In addition to all these, the book also includes 'Some few, (but choice) Physicall Receits [or medicines].' This variety of content does not seem to have disturbed the seventeenth- and eighteenth-century mind, for a number of books on painting methods include such information, most famous of which is William Salmon's *Polygraphice*, dedicated to 'Sᵣ Godf. Kneller Kt' and first published in 1701. This book enjoyed a considerable reputation in the eighteenth century. George Fisher's *The Instructor or Young Man's best Companion* and its various editions acknowledge under the heading 'Of Dialling' [sun dials] the 'sundry Mixtures of Colours and dying Stuffs, etc, collected from Mr *Salmon's Polygraphice*'.[5]

One of the earliest manuals in English to look exclusively at the methods employed by the visual artist was *The Art of Painting in Oyl* by John Smith C.M. [chemist]. This book was first published in 1671 but went through numerous editions into the nineteenth century.[6] It strongly echoes Cennino Cennini, unlike Smith's later work *The Art of Painting in Water Colours*.[7]

The fashion for lacquer in the late seventeenth century inevitably resulted in one of those 'Do It Yourself' books:

A Treatise of Japanning and Varnishing, being a complete Discovery of those Arts with the best way of making all sorts of Varnish for Japan Wood, Prints or Pictures, . . . Gilding, Burnishing, and Lackering with the Art of Gilding, Separating, and Refusing Metals and of Painting Mezzo-Tinto-Prints, Counterfeiting Tortoiseshell, and Marble, and for straining or Dying Wood, Ivory and Horn. Together with Above an Hundred distinct Patterns for Japan-work in imitation of the Indians, for Tables, Stands, Frames, Cabinets, Boxes, etc. Curiously Engraven on 24 large Copper-Plates.

This book was published in 1688 by John Stalker and George Parker and addressed itself primarily to those concerned with the new enthusiasm for 'Cathay' in interior decoration. A craft today is often seen as the product of one individual. This was not always true. More often than not an object would have been made by a whole series of craftsmen. A table designed by William Kent would have been constructed by a cabinet-maker and passed on to a carver to be finally 'cut in the white' (gesso), and then gilded by yet another specialist: a total of, in this instance, three craftsmen working for one designer. Stalker and Parker reflect this approach; each of their recipes and instructions concern but part of a continuing process.

Japanning became a fashionable pastime for ladies of leisure in the late seventeenth and early eighteenth centuries. Mrs Pendarves (later Mrs Delany) became something of an authority on the subject of japanning. 'Lady Sun [Sunderland, her sister] is very busy about japanning. I will perfect myself in the art against I make you a visit, and bring such materials with me', she wrote on 23 August 1729. And on 9 September 1729, 'Everybody is mad about japan work; I hope to be a dab at it by the time I see you.' A couple of years later she wrote again on 13 July 1713, 'You never saw such perfection as Mrs Clayton's trunk;

Designs for cabinet drawers from A Treatise on Japanning and Varnishing, *published in 1688 by John Stalker and George Parker.*

Left: *Patterns for powder boxes and patch boxes from* A Treatise on Japanning and Varnishing. *Above: An engraving by Jean Pillement for Robert Sayer's* The Ladies Amusement *(1760).*

other's Japan is beautiful, but this is *beauty*—it is the admiration of the whole town.'[8] Even when japanning had ceased to be fashionable for interior decoration it apparently remained a popular pastime. Robert Sayer's book *The Ladies Amusement or Whole Art of Japanning Made Easy* with engravings by Jean Pillement was published in London in 1760.

Handbooks continued to appear with increasing frequency, for a variety of motives. In the preface to his book *Handmaid to the Arts* (London 1764) Robert Dossie expressed the hope that it would inspire

> . . . the national improvement of skill and taste, in the execution of works of design, [which] is a matter of great importance to any country, not only on

account of the honour which is derived to civilized nations by excelling in the polite arts, but likewise of the commercial advantages resulting from it . . . .

Dossie appears to look back somewhat anxiously to the works of earlier writers. He makes comparisons, usually odious, between his own work and that of Count Caylas, Mr Muntz, Caneparius [de Atramentis], Merret's translation of Neri, and William Salmon. Dossie's book was not directed at the folk artist. It was however intended for those countries where

> The strong dispositon that prevails not only in European countries, but in the respective settlements of their people in Asia and America, for using those decorations and ornaments in dress, as well as in buildings, equipages, and furniture that employs the arts of design.

Many of these volumes were widely published. A book entitled *Valuable Secrets Concerning Arts and Trades* appeared in London in 1775, Dublin 1778, Norwich, Connecticut 1795, Boston 1798 and New York in 1809 and 1816.[9] Not all such books were designed for the artistic leisured, as for example 'Smith's *The Art of House Painting, improved by W. Butcher,*' (London, 1825).

An excellent example of the wide range of materials used in folk are – a Victorian seaweed basket: 'Call us not weeds, We are flowers of the sea'.

The materials used by folk artists were extraordinarily diverse. The two-dimensional work, in addition to the use of paint suspended in various media or 'vehicles', included textiles, wood veneers, seeds, straw, or several of these used simultaneously in one composition. The three-dimensional work that has survived is no less varied: carved wood and stone, wrought iron, tin and engraved ivory. The folk sculptor continued the tradition of using materials that were available in the locality in which he was working. In the eighteenth century, and even more so in the nineteenth, this distinguished his work from that of the 'respectable' sculptor who worked only in marble or bronze.

Painting

Oil paint sold in tubes was an innovation of the 1830's, like photography, and for its place in the history of art must rank in importance with the development of perspective in fifteenth-century Italy. Early in the nineteenth century it was possible to buy prepared paints in little bladders or small metal cylinders which dispensed their contents by means of a piston. Queen Victoria's paint-box in the Royal Academy contains examples of these.

Pigments Early painters ground their own pigments, using a pestle and mortar or a slab of marble. There is an example

of such a palette, of Purbeck marble, in the Roman City Museum at St Albans. '. . . grind all these things up well on a porphyry slab . . . and grind them as much as ever you can stand grinding them . . .' was Cennini's recommendation. John Smith also mentioned porphyry in this context in *The Art of Painting in Oyl* (1676). 'A Grinding stone and Mulier; the stone it self ought to be Porphyrie, which is the best . . .' It was important, as the 1705 edition stated, that the grindstone should '. . . not be spongy or full of small Pores . . .' Smith described the muller in the 1705 edition as 'a pebble Stone of the form of an Egg.'

Once the pigments were ground and mixed with a medium, care had to be taken to isolate them, to prevent evaporation or contamination by impurities. According to Cennini such colours should be put into a little jar and covered with 'clear river or fountain or well water; while Smith encouraged the use of bladders:

Queen Victoria's paint box made from inlaid wood. 20½in x 15in x 6in. The tortoiseshell lid is inscribed 'To my Beloved Victoria from her Affectionate Mother'. The box is fitted with cylindrical metal containers carrying the names of the pigments.

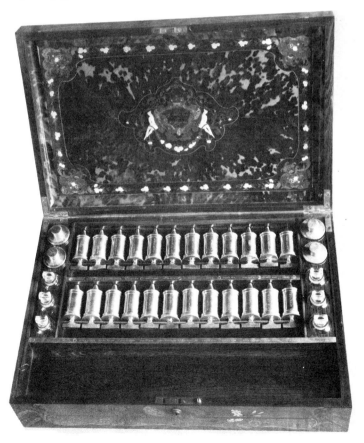

. . . a parcel of Colours given me in the Year 1661 by a Neighbouring Yeoman, that were as he said, left at his House by a Trooper that quartered there in the time of the Wars, about the year 1644. This Man was by Profession a Picture-Drawer, and his Colours were all tied up in Bladders . . . and when I opened them seventeen years later I found them in very good condition . . .*

As do most such works, Salmon's *Polygraphice* lists numerous preparations of mineral colours, for example:

To make a Mineral Yellow

Auri pigmentum, Leaf Silver mix, and grind them upon a Porphyry to an impalpable pouder, with water: which dry and keep for use. If Leaf Gold be ground with it, it will make two other sorts of Yellows: So also pure red Crocus Martis be added, in place of Gold. But as to proportions of these things, Reason and Experience must teach you.

Cennini describes how to make numerous colours but for vermilion he advises 'rather to get some of that which you find at the drugist for your money, so as not to lose time in the many variations of procedure as it is made by alchemy.' Significantly, he recommends that one should 'Always buy vermilion unbroken, and not pounded or ground' as 'it is generally adulterated, either with red lead or with pounded brick.' Various colours had to be ground in different ways, for example, 'A Green called Malachite' was 'For the sake of the colour' not to be ground too much or 'it would come out a dingy and ashy colour.' Ultramarine was made of lapis lazuli that was pounded 'in a bronze mortar, covered up so that it may not go off in dust.'

To ensure the fineness of the various powder colours, sieves were used. 'They should be made of pewter, in the form of the common earthen cullenders, but with more and larger holes'; in addition it was necessary to 'strain it through a linen cloth or rather filtering paper.'[5] Stalker and Parker describe a method of suspending pigment in water to select the finest powder.

Fill one of your [four or five wine] glasses with [clear water] put in half an Ounce, or as much of your colour as you intend to wash; stir it well about with your knife, permit it to stand no longer than while you could count or tell forty; and in this short space of time all the coarse will sink and settle to the bottom, the finer remains floating in the water . . .

Dossie describes 'The operation subservient to the making and preparing colours [as] sublimation, calcination, solu-tion, precipitation, filtration, and levigation.'[10]

Apart from mineral or earth colours the 'Preparations of Vegitable Colours' were also important; for example, a recipe for a scarlet from Kermes berries was described by William Salmon with the final recommendation to 'take it up with an Ivory Spoon, make it up into cakes and keep it for use. It is an excellent Lake.' The *Polygraphice* goes on to describe how to make tinctures or lakes from poppies, 'flower-de-luces', red roses, violets, green herbs, borage flowers, carnations, cowslips and colworts.

Media In grinding many of these colours, water or some other medium was customarily added. For example, 'take some Bagdad indigo, and work it up very thoroughly with water . . . to make an imitation Azurite.'[1] The media were accordingly not simply seen as carrying agents. The medium for a paint usually contains two functions in one: a carrying agent, and a binding agent which fixes the colour. Sometimes the underpainting was executed in paint with a carrying medium that was 'lean' in character, for example tempera, and the overpainting was carried out in oil paint that was 'fatty' in character: a sound principle still observed by house painters. Many sorts of media were employed and some were particularly appropriate to certain colours. 'A colour which is made of Azurite and Giallorino is green . . . it is tempered with yolk of egg',[1] that is to say, tempera. Some colours which were ground with clear water, such as white lead, were regarded as being 'compatible with any tempera.'[1]

Of all the media used in painting, watercolour was perhaps the most easily made but the most difficult to use. 'Gambogia or Gutta Gamba', for example, 'easily desolves in Water, and makes a yellow staining Liquor to wash pictures and maps with.'[5] Dossie includes a section in his book entitled 'Of the substances used for rending water a proper vehicle for colours'. This chapter is concerned with watercolour as the medium for miniature painting, and the binding agents that Dossie suggests for this purpose include 'Gum Arabic', 'Gum Senegal', 'Sugar' and 'Sugar-Candy', 'Starch', 'Isinglass', and 'Size', which he described as 'leather boild in water til it becomes of a viscid consis-tence'.[10]

Turpentine is a resin derived from various conifers. A number of different turpentines were in use, among them 'the Common Venetian, Strasburg, Cyprus and Chio' and of these the Venetian, an exudate of larch, was most recom-

*It is tempting to speculate about this 'Picture-Drawer'. Could he have been William Dobson (1610-1646), about whom so little is known?

Right: *The Sun, painted in oil on a softwood panel and oil gilded; it bears the initials T.M., probably those of the licensee.*

mended but it was important to '*chuse* that which is whitest clearest and finest.'[5]

Related to the turpentines were the lacquers, listed by Salmon: 'gum-lac, called shell-lac, gum-animi (it is either Oriental, coming from the East Indies or Occidental, coming from the West Indies), gum copal (from Hispaniola, Cuba and other places in the Spanish West Indies), gum sandarack (brought from Barbary in long Tears or Drops), benjamine, rosin, mastiche (gum of the lentisk tree growing in Chio, Egypt and Syria), gum-elemi' and finally the mysterious 'olibanum' which was 'the true ancient Incence but from what tree it is produced, Authors have not agreed'. However, Salmon goes on to say 'but for myself being in the West Indies, I gathered it plentifully from the Floridian Cedar which is the cedrus baccifera.'[5] All of these lacquers were used in a variety of ways for both varnishing and japanning.

Not all colours will dry equally readily. Stalker and Parker point out that 'Red Orpiment you must mix with drying Oyl' and Salmon gives two methods of making such oil:

> Mix Linseed Oil in a quart with litharge of gold and boil them for a quarter of an hour; if you would have it more drying, boil it a while longer, but have care of boiling it till it is too thick, and unfit for use.

Milk was occasionally used as a medium but from ancient (e.g. Romano–Egyptian) times wax was even more important. Edward Edwards in his *Anecdotes of the Painters* (1808) mentions this method in connection with the artist J. H. Muntz:

> . . . he had a landscape painted in *encaustic* a process of which he seems to have considered himself the inventor; for he published a small octavo volume (1760) in which he demonstrated the operation, but it certainly does not deserve the attention of an artist.

The luminosity of this type of painting is the result of the ability of the underlying material to shine through the pigment. This process is particularly effective for interior woodwork.

Painting Surfaces　Paint has been applied on numerous surfaces, and just as the painter traditionally but not exclusively used a flat surface, so the sculptor traditionally though not exclusively painted his three-dimensional work. Some pigments and some media are more suitable for particular

Left: A carved and painted wooden gunsmith's store figure, from the second quarter of the 18th century. The gun incorporates a real flintlock mechanism shown in greater detail on page 25.

The sign of The Brazen George, painted on cast iron and removed from its site in Cambridge in 1850.

surfaces. The flexible nature of oil paint, for example, makes it especially appropriate for application to canvas. The wood panel (and the ancon), wall, iron, parchment, stone and glass are all surfaces referred to by Cennini, and to these should be added marble, slate, copper and tin.

The Wall　Since true fresco depended for its survival upon a dry climate, this activity of painting in watercolour on a damp plaster surface was generally confined to those countries bordering the Mediterranean. Painting on dry plaster (*fresco secco*) was practiced in northern Europe as in America, where this subject has been studied extensively. Post-medieval and pre-Victorian examples of pictorial walls, and some examples of patterned walls, produced with the aid of stencils, have recently been discovered in Britain. These seem to have been done in watercolour directly on dry, fresh plaster. The methods used in Britain appear to be similar to those employed in America, where Rufus Porter and J. H. Warner were great exponents of the art of wall

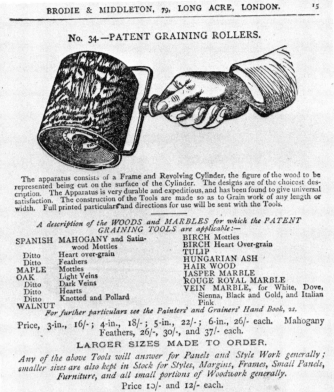

No. 34.—PATENT GRAINING ROLLERS.

The apparatus consists of a Frame and Revolving Cylinder, the figure of the wood to be represented being cut on the surface of the Cylinder. The designs are of the choicest description. The Apparatus is very durable and expeditious, and has been found to give universal satisfaction. The construction of the Tools are made so as to Grain work of any length or width. Full printed particulars and directions for use will be sent with the Tools.

A description of the WOODS and MARBLES for which the PATENT GRAINING TOOLS are applicable:—

SPANISH MAHOGANY and Satin-wood Metties		BIRCH Mottles
		BIRCH Heart Over-grain
Ditto	Heart over-grain	TULIP
Ditto	Feathers	HUNGARIAN ASH
MAPLE	Mottles	HAIR WOOD
OAK	Light Veins	JASPER MARBLE
Ditto	Dark Veins	ROUGE ROYAL MARBLE
Ditto	Hearts	VEIN MARBLE, for White, Dove,
Ditto	Knotted and Pollard	Sienna, Black and Gold, and Italian
WALNUT		Pink

For further particulars see the Painters' and Grainers' Hand Book, 2s.

Price, 3-in., 16/-; 4-in., 18/-; 5-in., 22/-; 6-in., 26/- each. Mahogany Feathers, 26/-, 30/-, and 37/- each.

LARGER SIZES MADE TO ORDER.

Any of the above Tools will answer for Panels and Style Work generally; smaller sizes are also kept in Stock for Styles, Margins, Frames, Small Panels, Furniture, and all small portions of Woodwork generally.

Price 10/- and 12/- each.

---

painting. The former, apart from his many other activities, founded the *Scientific American*, and there he describes the methods that were used for stencilling. His surviving stencils were cut with wood-carving tools from heavy gauge paper, stiffened with varnish and the strength gained from many layers of paint, the result of constant use. The pigments were 'mixt with strong beer or milk',[11] although lampblack was sometimes mixed with water and rum. Stencilling was also sometimes used to decorate wallpaper, rather than being applied direct to the wall surface. Dossie gives the following account:

> The manner of stencilling the colours is this. The figure, which all the parts of any particular colour make in the design to be printed is to be cut out, in a piece of this leather [probably parchment] or oilcloth. These pieces of leather or oilcloth are called stencils, and being laid flat on sheets of paper to be printed, spread on a table or floor, are rubbed over with the colour properly tempered, by means of a large brush. The colour passing over the whole is consequently spread on those parts of the paper where the cloth or leather is cut away, and give the same effect as if laid on by a print. This is nevertheless only practicable without great care in parts where there are only de-

Left: *Stencilled wallpaper from Holly Tree House, Colchester (c1750).* Above: *A patent graining roller with a list of the woods and marbling effects available as advertised for sale in* The Practical Carver and Gilder's Guide and Picture Frame Maker's Companion (*Brodie & Middleton, 79 Longacre and Simpkin, Marshall & Co., Stationers' Hall Court*).

> tached masses or spots of colours; for where there are small lines, or parts that run one into another, it is difficult to preserve the connection or continuity of the parts of the cloth, or to keep the smaller corners close down to the paper, and therefore in such cases prints are preferable. Stencilling is indeed a cheaper method of ridding coarse work than printing . . .

Plank panelling (also known in America as feather-edge sheathing); the more sophisticated panels set in styles and rails; even the humble match-boarding: all these have been embellished with decorative painting. It was common practice to paint a simple wood with the grain of a more handsome species and it was 'Recommended that all woodwork if possible be grained in imitation of some natural wood, not with a view of having the imitation mistaken for the original but rather to create an allusion to it, and by a diversity of lines to produce a kind of variety and intricacy which affords more pleasure to the eye than a flat shade of colour'.[12] Walls panelled with wood were however also marbled or painted to counterfeit tortoiseshell. In Jacobean times, the medieval tradition for painted decoration of a pictorial sort persisted, a tradition that was in a sense maintained by the fashion for things oriental, and panelling painted in imitation of oriental lacquer occasionally appeared in the late seventeenth centuries.

Panel Painting The methods used in preparing and painting interior panelling were much the same as those used for painting a panel for a pub sign or a sundial. Salmon's *Polygraphice* gives the following instructions in Book III, Chapter 17:

Of Painting Sun Dials, Timber-work, etc

i)   . . . make of the firmest and clearest Oak, and thoroughly dry.

ii)   Cut your board to such a length as you intend the length of the dial to be of and so many of them, as make up the designed breadth; joynt and plain them on both sides, then set them to dry (for they have lain in a House ever so long, and are never so dry, yet thus shot and plained, they will *shrink* afterwards beyond belief).

iii)   When they are dry enough, and will shrink no more, *shote* them again with good Joynts, which fasten together in glewing with Pins or Pegs, as Coopers do the bottoms of their tubs.

iv)   Being thus glewed and dryed, let it be well plained and tryed every way that it may be smooth and true; let the edges be shot true, and all of a thickness, that they may fit into the Rabets of the Mouldings, put round it just as a panel of Wainscot doth in its Frame.

v)   This will give the board liberty to shrink and swell without rending, whereas mouldings nailed round the edges, as the vulgar way is, doth so restrain the motion of the Wood, that it cannot shrink without tearing; but made this way, they will last a long time without either parting in the Joynts, or splitting in the Wood.

Such panels, and indeed carved wood shop signs, roundabout horses and ships' figureheads, would first be 'prepared'.

The Knots especially of fir, in painting new work, will destroy its good effect if they be not first properly "*killed*", as the painters term it. The best way of effecting this is by laying upon those knots which retain any turpentine a considerable substance of lime immediately after it is slaked . . . it is then scraped off,

and the knots must be painted over with what is called *size knotting*, a composition of red and white lead ground very fine with water on a stone, and mixed with strong double glue size, and use warm.

So strong are the craft traditions that one can almost hear the voice of Cennini in these instructions from Gwilt's *Encyclopaedia of Architecture* (new edition, London, 1876). Gwilt continues:

When the knotting is completed, the *priming colour* is laid on. The priming colour is composed of white and a little red lead mixed thin with linseed oil. One pound of it will cover from 18 to 20 yards.

A second coat of the primer mixed with an equal proportion of the final colour should then be applied and 'The work should now remain for some days to harden.'

The *Polygraphice* states that:

The colors chiefly made use of in painting Dials are 1 Ceruse, 2 White Lead, 3 Lamp Black 4 Char Coal or Sea Coal, 5 Spanish-Brown, 6 Red Lead, 7 Vermilion, 8 Cinnaber Lake, 9 Smalt, 10 Blew Bice, 11 Blew Verditer, 12 Indigo, 13 Umber, 14 Verdigrise, 15 Yellow Oaker, 16 Yellow Pink. But if you will have your Dial more rich you must have Leaf Gold [which for outdoor use was of course laid with oil-based gold size].

Salmon goes on to explain that 'To paint Wainscot, Doors', etc, 'This differs not much from the former method of Painting Sun-Dials.' In addition to these oil-based paints I have seen examples of simple distemper being used to decorate interior woodwork.

The Panel & the Canvas

But still I must get back to our painting, and from the wall go on to panels or anconas, the nicest and neatest occupation which we have in our profession.[1]

The above goes far to suggest that even in Cennini's day the easel painting was beginning to assume some dominance, though the sub-culture of folk art remained free of this sense of cultural superiority.[13]

In preparing a surface to take paint it is necessary to provide some means of bonding the paint to the base surface, be it canvas, wood, stone or metal. For this purpose size of various sorts is employed. Size, being an animal glue of boiled bones, skin (for example, rabbit skin) or parchment, is liable to mildew, so 'to keep it from going bad, put in some salt.'[1] While speaking of sizes and glues, it is worth noting that Cennini alludes to 'a glue used by workers in wood; this is made of cheese . . . with a little quicklime.' This must have been an early form of casein glue well known to craftsmen. In *Nollekens and his Times* J. T. Smith[14] mentions that '. . . Mr. Roubiliac, when he had to mend a broken antique [marble] would mix grated Gloucester cheese with his plaster, adding the grounds of porter and the yoke of an egg; which mixture when dry forms a very hard cement . . .' John Smith (C.M.) states that 'Glew [and size] is always melted in a Balneo Maria which is this; Take a large Skillet, or a little Kettle full of water, into which put your Glew-pot with a wispe of Hay or Straw under it to keep it from the bottom . . .' The use of the double saucepan prevented the glue or size from overheating.

Most of the recommendations in these old manuals are still valid, though it is difficult, if not impossible, to maintain such high standards today when the ingredients are often unobtainable. The wood selected for a panel painting should be well seasoned, close grained and free from knots; in Italy this included woods such as 'poplar of good quality, or of linden [lime tree] or willow'.[1] Salmon, in his instructions 'To make Tortoise Shell Japan' where the preparation was much the same, mentions woods available in England: 'let your wood be close grained, smooth, and well wrought, as Box, Pear Tree, Walnut Tree, etc. (However, many a Russian or Greek icon was painted successfully on the coarsest fir.) Salmon goes on to recommend that 'if it be coarse grained, as Deal, Oak, etc, you must prime it with size or whitening.' But, as Stalker and Parker confirm, it was preferable if '. . . your wood . . . be close grained, exempt and free from all knots and greasiness, very smooth, clean and well rush't.' (Dutch rushes were used to smooth over wood or gesso work, and are further discussed in the following section.) Apart from making sure that the wood is well seasoned, special attention should be given to any knots that persist. Flaws in the timber such as knots or even nail heads can be made good by a mixture of strong size and sawdust.[1] 'Keep your work always warm, by no means hot', so that the first coat of thin size will soak into the wood and dry well. This size is best made from sheep parchments or rabbit skin and its strength when melted down in a pot over a flame may be tested 'with the palms of your hands'[1] or the thumb and index finger, 'and when you find that one palm sticks to the other it will be right.'[1] The first coat should be one part of this size with two parts water, the next two parts size, one water and the final coat should be the full strength.

At this stage alternatives appear; painters demanding a 'tooth' to work on usually apply fine linen soaked in size; wood sculptors with cracks to cover up often apply strips of linen over such inequalities in the same manner. The icons of the Orthodox Churches of eastern Europe, the panels and ancones of the Italian primitives and the wood sculptures of medieval Europe in general used linen as a base for subsequent coats of gesso. This preparation was not essential and eighteenth-century English gesso mirrors and furniture survive in great numbers, although the gesso was applied for the most part direct on the wood. Gesso is composed of a mixture of whitening (not plaster of Paris) and size. The first coats should be strong in size and weak in whitening. 'Melt some [size] over a gentle fire and scrape into it as much whiting as may only colour it', is how Salmon phrases it. Each subsequent coat should be progressively weaker in size and stronger and thicker in whitening.

Carved work should be re-established with carving tools to 'open up the veins of the carved-work which the Whiting has Choakt up; then with a fine Rag wetted and [on] your finger, carefully smooth . . .'[5] Gesso work is best done in warm, dry weather and of the ten to fifteen coats of gesso each should be permitted to dry thoroughly, the final coats needing more time than the earlier layers. Once the gesso has 'come out like ivory'[1] the panel is ready to be worked on by the painter. Size and whitening of much the same mixture is also applied to canvases as a primer. The stretcher or, as it was known in the eighteenth century, the 'straining frame' should be well bevelled on the arrises that are adjacent to the canvas, otherwise a 'ghost' of the stretcher eventually appears. Salmon recommends that the canvas should first be smoothed over with a 'Slick-Stone' and that 'the Primed Cloath' should have its first coats of size and its subsequent coats of whitening and size mixed 'with a little honey', insisting that 'honey keeps it from cracking, peeling or breaking out'. This may well be the case, but perhaps it should be pointed out here that Salmon was a doctor of medicine at a time when medicine was only beginning to emerge as a science; much of the *Polygraphice* is concerned with positively alarming 'cures' for all manner of complaints, including cancer!

Gilding

The three basic methods of gilding are by water, oil and fire. Fire-gilding was for use on metal, usually bronze, but such fine decoration—ormolu—was for the most sophisticated work and accordingly does not concern us.

Water-gilding was the finest method of gilding materials other than metal, but was, unlike oil-gilding, only suitable for interior use. The great advantage of this method is that it can be burnished. The wood to be water-gilt is first prepared with gesso and smoothed over as described for panel painting. As gold or silver will reveal the slightest unevenness in the surface, especially if the work is to be burnished, this smoothing over should be thoroughly done. This may be achieved by rubbing the surface with a damp piece of linen on the forefinger. Carvers have always avoided the use of sandpaper or glasspaper due to the tendency of small particles of sand or glass to be left behind disrupting gilding or blunting the carving tools. For this reason, sharkskin was used as an abrasive, and a number of manuals including the *Polygraphice* and the *Treatise* refer to Dutch rushes. The rush here refers to 'the stalk or hollow stem-like leaves of several plants . . . large quantities of the "horse-tail", *Equisetum hiemale*, are used under the name of Dutch or scouring rush for scouring metal and other hard surfaces on account of the large proportion of silica the plant contains.'[15] The gold size for water-gilding consists of Armenian bole, a red earth, mixed with water and warmed over a flame to blood heat with a small quantity of size, although Salmon suggests the addition of 'a little tried beef Suet'. For water-gilding silver, tobacco-pipe clay took the place of the Armenian bole and again, according to Salmon, 'Deers Suet' or Genoa Soap' (Stalker and Parker suggest 'Castile-soap') took the place of beef suet. Once the bole is dry, 'wet such another part of your work and lay on your gold . . . If your work be sufficiently moist, you'll perceive how lovingly the gold will embrace it.' The newly applied gold is then left so that the bole may dry once again, after which you may burnish your work. 'A Dog's tooth

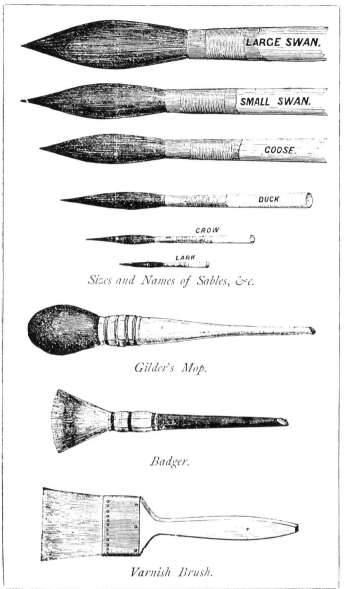

Sizes and Names of Sables, &c.

Gilder's Mop.

Badger.

Varnish Brush.

Above: *A page advertising gilder's brushes from* The Practical Carver and Gilder's Guide and Picture Frame Maker's Companion.
Left: *A gilder's cushion from the same handbook.*

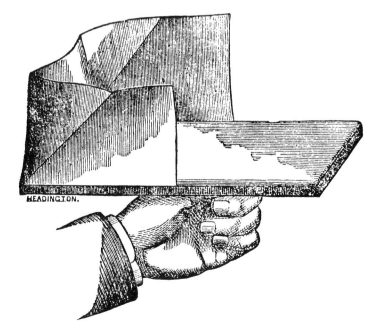

HEADINGTON.

was formerly lookt upon as the fittest instrument for this business; but of late agguts and Pebbles are more highly esteemed.'[4]

Water-gilding, as has been seen, is an immensely skilled process, and was not much practised by the folk artists of provincial Britain. Oil gilding, on the other hand, was common. Apart from the ease with which this method of gilding may be accomplished, it has the added advantage that it may be used for exterior work, on anything from inn signs to railings.

The gold size for oil gilding was made of 'Yellow Oker in fine powder . . . mixt with Linseed Oil, which is somewhat fat.'[5] According to the degree of 'fatiness' the size will vary in the time that it takes to set sufficiently to be suitable for the application of either loose-leaf or transfer gold. Loose-leaf gold is customarily used only indoors, and is cut while the work progresses on a cushion or pad covered with suede and protected from draughts at one end by a parchment fence 'to keep their leaves of Gold from Wind and Air.'[5]

Brushes & Other Tools

Today the word 'pencil' is exclusively applied to the lead pencil, but the word traditionally referred to the brush, principally that used by artists. A great variety of brushes were used and among the earliest were undoubtedly those which nature herself provides, and which continue in use to this day. Salmon refers to 'Varnishing Pencils' of camel's hair and to 'Drawing Pencils both greater and lesser, as great-Goose, little Goose, Duck, Crow and Swallow Quills', which were apparently conventional hair brushes set in a ferrule formed by a quill. He goes on to say that, for drawing, 'the longest haired pencils are the best.' The size of the feather indicated the size of the brush, thus larger brushes used swans' quills.

> In chusing pencils . . . put them into your mouth, and moisten them a little, then draw them forth between the Tongue and Lip, and if they come out with an intire sharp point, without cleaving in twain, they are good . . .[7]

Special brushes were needed for gilding including a 'tip' made of—

> A squirrel's tail . . . for taking up whole leaves [of gold] . . . [it] is cut short, and sometimes spread in a fan-fashion by means of a piece of wood formed like a pencil stick, but broad at one end, and split to receive the tail . . .[10]

Paint and varnishes were often mixed and kept in mussel-shells. They were used in great numbers, '2 or 3 hundred . . . not that you will need a tenth part of them at once, but you might seek them when you want them.' Surely always good advice to those artists and craftsmen with capital! The artist's palette has assumed an almost heraldic significance, and the word itself a more than metaphoric importance. Many eighteenth-century palettes were not of

the familiar shape but were: rectangular, with a handle. The fashionable portrait painter travelling from mansion to mansion carried his fragile glass bottles containing precious oils from place to place in turned boxwood containers. Other equipment included 'an Easel . . . easie to make by your self or by a Joyner; it must be almost after the fashion of a Ladder about 7 feet high,'[16] a 'Pantograph formerly called a parallelogram, and by some at present a Mathematical compas'.[10] For 'drawing after nature' the 'camera obscura of which a portable kind adapted to this purpose is commonly made by opticians,'[10] was also used.

Examples of 'writers' and 'pencils' from The Practical Carver and Gilder's Guide

No. 77.—CAMEL-HAIR WRITERS.

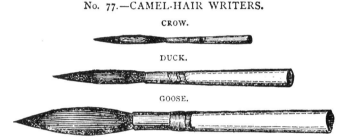

Crow, 8/-; Duck, 10/-; Goose, 12/-. Assorted, 10/- gross.

No. 78.—CAMEL-HAIR JAPANNERS' LONG WRITERS.

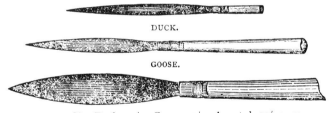

Crow, 8/-; Duck, 10/-; Goose, 12/-; Assorted, 10/- gross.

No. 79.—CAMEL-HAIR SWAN PENCILS.

Small, 18/-; Large, 24/-.

No. 80.—CAMEL-HAIR SWAN TINS.

24/- gross. Ex. Large, 42/-.

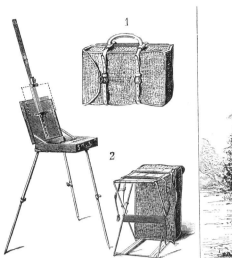

Mechanical Methods of drawing Landscapes, &c.

Printed for J. Hinton in Newgate Street.

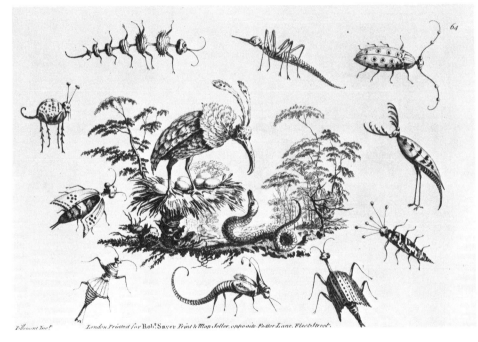

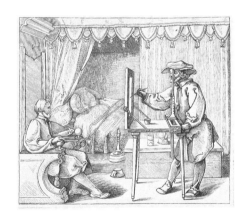

Top: '*Useful Equipment for the Itinerant Artist*', an engraving from a French publication of 1885.
Above: *An engraving by Jean Pillement from Robert Sayer's* The Ladies Amusement.

Various methods were devised to trace engravings from copybooks like those in *The Ladies Amusement* by Jean Pillement.

> It is advised by some to use paper made transparent by means of oil of turpentine instead of the tiffany and lawn (the equivalent of architects' linen) . . . the paper

Top right: '*Mechanical methods of drawing landscapes, &c.*' a copper plate engraving in The Universal Magazine, *April 1755*.
Right: *Woodcut by Durer showing the use of mathematical instruments to assist in portrait painting.*

> employed for this purpose should be called fan-paper, which is to be had at the fan-makers . . .[10]

A design recorded in this way could then be transferred by means of pricking and pouncing.

> This method is called calking, and is performed also in

23

another way, by puncturing or pricking the original print or drawing, and producing an outline on a new ground, by transmitting a coloured powder through the punctured holes . . .[10]

Easels, mall-sticks and diminishing-glasses completed the effects of the painter's studio whatever his status: professional, amateur or that of the homely sign writer, from whose numbers so many folk artists emerged.

Carving

Many of the crafts involving the application of paint or gold leaf to a variety of surfaces require the knowledge of a series of recipes which, with intelligence, may be prepared and used by all. The skills that are demanded for carving in wood and stone may not be reduced to a series of instructions. The printed word alone cannot explain how a wood-carving gouge should be held, and not even a photograph can demonstrate how a pitching-hammer should strike the pitcher. The degree of skill that wood-carving and stone-carving require may be acquired only by at least seven years' apprenticeship from an early age. The so-called general education can be said, therefore, to have destroyed these and many other crafts, particularly the carving of wood which, contrary to popular belief, is a more difficult material to handle than stone.

Wood-carving   In the whole history of art one can associate the name of very few 'great' sculptors with the use of wood; perhaps they were too busy developing at a philosophical level to become accomplished in such a difficult craft. The folk sculptors, on the other hand, have more often worked in wood than in stone.

Most wood sculpture is the work of professionals who, necessarily, are professionally equipped. The carver's bench is traditionally 38 inches high, whereas the maker's bench is 33 inches. A wood-carver needs at least one hundred wood-carving tools; in fact three hundred is a likelier figure. This is because each curve in the tool must correspond to the form that is to be cut; it is not usually possible to create a concave or convex form with a flat chisel, as in stone-carving.

Sharpening such tools is an immensely skilful business. The wood-carver must have a large stock of 'slips', or stones shaped to sharpen specific curves. A strop is also necessary to remove the 'burr' occasioned by sharpening on the stone. Some tools could take an hour or more to sharpen sufficiently to cut a softwood 'sweetly' across the grain. All European wood-carvers, with the exception of the Florentines, sharpen their tools both on the 'outside' and on the 'inside', in contrast to the 'makers' whose chisels are bevelled on one

A rack of tools belonging to the Bristol carver, A. E. Anderson.

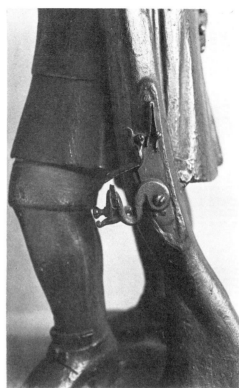

Above: *A selection of 18th century wood carver's tools now in the Victoria & Albert Museum.*
Right: *Flintlock mechanism of the gun held by the figure shown opposite page 17.*

side only. Paradoxically, the softer the wood, the more difficult the technique and the sharper the tool should be. Consequently oak is, up to a point, an easier wood to carve than pine. Grinling Gibbons wove his near excesses of skill not into a softwood but into a reasonably soft hardwood: lime. This means that the wood-carver takes up a position somewhat the reverse of the cabinet-maker, for whom the softwoods are easier to handle.

The work of the wood-carver was often painted, and for this reason it was not necessary to produce figure work from bulky timbers, for laminated bodies and jointed limbs would not show under paint. A further advantage was that arms and legs could be constructed with the grain running along them, thus not necessitating the use of the fragile 'short' grain.

The wood-carvings produced by amateurs seldom approached the subtleties of form acquired by the professionals. Chip carving, with its simple methods and the discipline imposed by these methods, permitted amateurs to produce pleasing and often complex results.

Stone Most parts of the world provide craftsmen with stone, marble or granite. Where wood is available it is usually most favoured, especially if an intractable material such as granite is the alternative. In the alluvial areas of the Fens, wood was almost the only material available and in medieval times was used to construct the fine Moot Halls financed by the civic pride of wool-wealth, although stone or clunch was used for ecclesiastical buildings. Even in the stone districts of England, the timber-framed building was once commonplace. However, by the eighteenth century, stone was the predominant material in regions such as the Cotswolds, and it is in these districts that some examples of the work of the folk artists in stone may be found.

Masons customarily work on low benches, or 'bankers', with the work below the swing of the 'mall' for economy of energy. The sculptor, on the other hand, usually likes to be on the same level as his work the better to see it; his mallet (diminutive of mall) is much lighter. The sculptor may also use a $2\frac{1}{2}$-lb hammer of iron (sometimes brass) or even a dummy (small mallet) of lead. Wood, iron, brass and lead are all materials that provide a non-jarring knock. However a pitching-hammer which is used by masons and sculptors when 'roughing out' work is usually of mild steel, as this is used in conjunction with a pitcher to knock large lumps of stone away with a staccato action. Gouges are seldom

The Moot Hall at Elstow, Bedfordshire, seen from the West.

used in stone-carving, and then only on the softer stones or free stones, like Bath stone. 'Quirks' were used to chase narrow channels, as in the folds of drapery, for which the bow drill was also used to great effect. The bow drill is an exceedingly sensitive implement and much more effective than any other type of drill for all manner of purposes.

Imported marble used in Britain by the 'academic' sculptor required a quite different technique from stone, with different tools. Preliminary form is established in stone with a 'punch', and in marble with a 'point'. Marble requires to be peeled away, a technique necessitating tools that have been finely 'drawn out' by the whitesmith.

Pointing-machine   Various methods of establishing a point in space have been used either to enlarge or to diminish sketch models, or to transfer a design from a plaster master to the permanence of wood or stone. The pointing-machine serves this purpose and is for the sculptor the equivalent of the pantograph or the 'squaring up' used by the painter. Such a slavish approach to sculpture was never adopted by folk artists, who were their own craftsmen. Many Victorian sculptors were incapable of carving and were dependent upon commercial carvers using a pointing-machine. Regrettably even Rodin was guilty of this procedure, a ploy to which no self-respecting ship carver sank! Surely this is one of the strengths of this 'naïve' work: the unity of purpose, means, conception and material.

By the late eighteenth century it was accepted that the fashionable sculptor simply produced a clay model:

I cannot suffer the uninformed reader to conclude, that the carver's powers are not absolutely requisite to the fame of the designer and modeller; for, without his tasteful finishing, the most exquisite model may be totally deprived of its feeling . . . What an acquisition, then, an excellent carver must be in the studio of the classic Sculptor of high fame, whose mind must necessarily be engaged upon his designs; and whose hand had it once been master of the tool, for want of practice, could not manage it with so much ease as that of the artist who is continually employed on the marble only . . .[14]

1 C. d'A. Cennini, *The Craftsman's Handbook*, trans. D. V. Thompson, Yale University Press, 1933.
2 *Oxford Companion to Art*, ed. H. Osborne, Clarendon Press, 1970.
3 Theophilus, *De Diversis Artibus*, trans. C. R. Dodwell, 1961.
4 John Stalker and George Parker, *A Treatise of Japaning*, Oxford, 1688.
5 William Salmon, *Polygraphice*, 1701. *The Instructors or A Young Man's Best Companion* by George Fisher. The John Judkyn Memorial Collection, Bath, includes a copy of the sixteenth edition, purchased by Benjamin Franklin in Bath in 1761, and also what appears to be a pirate edition published in Walpole, New Hampshire, in 1794 by Isaiah Thomas and David Carlisle.
6 *e.g. The Art of Painting in Oil*, published by R. H. Laurie, 1827.
7 John Smith, C.M., *The Art of Painting in Water Colours*. This book also went through numerous editions. The author has consulted the 1730 edition 'Printed in London for, and Sold by Mary Smith, at the *Fan* and *Flower-de-Luce* over against *Somerset House* in the *Strand* and no where else'.
8 *The Autobiography and Correspondence of Mary Granville, Mrs Delany*, ed. Lady Llanover, 1st series, 1861.
9 See *Antiques* magazine, June 1942, *Art Instruction Books for the People* by Carl W. Drepperd. This article is mainly concerned with American publications, mostly of the nineteenth century, although many of the books listed in Drepperd's bibliography were in fact first published in Britain, i.e. *The Oxford Drawing Book* by Nathaniel Whittock, London, 1825, New York 1842.
10 Robert Dossie, *The Handmaid to the Arts*, London, 1764, vol. 1, chapter II, section II.
11 *Bulletin of the Connecticut Historical Society*, January 1943, quoting a document of 1801.
12 J. C. Loudon, *An Encyclopaedia of Cottage, Farm and Villa Architecture and Furniture* (first published in London, 1836).
13 See also 'How from the wall you enter upon panel-painting', Cennini.
14 J. T. Smith, *Nollekens and his Times*, vol. II, 1919 ed. (First published 1829.)
15 *Encyclopaedia Britannica*, 11th ed, 1910.
16 J. T. Smith (see 14).

Ecce Signum

It is well known that Hogarth painted inn signs, but then it is likely that such contact with this social and artistic level gave him much of the vitality that he portrayed. J. T. Smith in *Nollekens and his Times*, first published in 1829, refers to a number of academic artists who produced carriage paintings and inn signs. He mentions, for example, 'Mr Smirke, the celebrated artist, [who] also served his time under an heraldic painter . . .' and George Morland, who painted a sign of a White Lion for a public house in Paddington.

While the work of these artists falls outside the scope of this book, some of their topographical views have provided us with valuable information concerning the appearance of English high streets in the eighteenth century while they were 'dressed overall' with inn, shop and trade signs. In contrast, nineteenth-century photographs of country towns show a remarkably drab scene in the absence of signs. Then as now many of the inn signs had declined to nothing but a lettered board bearing, for example, the words 'The Sun' rather than its actual representation.

Signs advertising various trades are known to have been used in antiquity by the Egyptians, Greeks and Romans. Surviving Roman examples are carved in stone or marble and once advertised a variety of shops including the shoemaker, baker, dairy and wine merchant. The Roman use

A mid-18th century engraving of Cheapside showing the multitude of shop and inn signs.

Inn Signs

Today the signboards for the inns and public houses of Britain are virtually the sole such embellishment to be found in our high streets. Of all such signs, it is the inn sign that has the longest history. In medieval Europe the manor and monastery alike, in common with Middle Eastern custom, regarded hospitality for travellers as a sacred duty. Accordingly most monastic settlements included a hospice as part of the complex of buildings, while in remote areas, en route to a place of pilgrimage such as Canterbury, a hospice not found in association with monastic buildings was provided by the church, such as the hospital at Maidstone founded by Archbishop Boniface in 1260.

The inn was the natural successor of the hospice, and thus provided food, drink and lodging, in contrast to the public house which did not provide lodging. Time and the progressively more nomadic quality of twentieth-century life has eroded these distinctions. There was also the medieval alehouse, well described in Langland's *Piers The Plowman* and in Skelton's *Elynor Rummynge*.

The origin of the inn sign is obscure. Undoubtedly the evergreen bush of Roman times continued in use, and these

This photograph of a saddler's shop in North Somerset, c1900, shows a fine shop sign of a carved carthorse in harness, with many of the saddler's wares on display.

Signboard for The White Hart, Witley, Surrey, painted c1875. The bracket has a gap at the far end where a bunch of grapes would have hung.

of an evergreen bush hung outside an inn persisted in medieval Europe; hence the proverb 'Good wine needs no bush'. The development of heraldry in the middle ages for the use of the Lords spiritual and temporal inevitably led, on the dissolution of the monasteries, to the use of such devices to advertise as an inn what had previously been the monastic hospice.

The History of Signboards by Jacob Larwood[1] and John Camden Hotten was first published in 1866 and remains one of the best books on the subject. Even at that date the authors regretted

> . . . that such a task [of recording surviving signboards] was not undertaken many years ago; it would have been better accomplished then than now . . . Already, during the printing of this work, three old houses famous for their signs have been doomed to destruction . . . The Mitre in Fleet Street, The Tabard in Southwark . . . and Don Saltero's house in Cheyne Walk, Chelsea. The best existing specimen of old signboards may be seen in our Cathedral towns.

bushes (or alternatively evergreen garlands or wreaths) were attached to long poles projecting from the tavern. By 1375 these poles had become so extravagant that it became necessary in London for the authorities to restrict their length to seven feet.[2] These signs were generic in character and served to indicate that a particular building was an inn, rather as the carved wood bunch of grapes was used at a later date to terminate the wrought-iron bracket that supported signs bearing a variety of devices.

An additional emblem became necessary to denote a particular inn, and Larwood and Hotten have suggested that the inn signs derive from the emblems displayed on the town houses of the 'inns' of noblement, 'inn' being a form of 'within', as in 'Inns of Court'. It has been suggested that the popular sign of the Chequers is derived from the coat of arms of the Earl of Arundel, but other authorities state that this sign was in common use with the Romans.[3] By 1393 it was unlawful for an innkeeper to trade without a sign, and in that year Florence North, a brewer in Chelsea, London, was prosecuted for not displaying one. This law was applied elsewhere, for in an Act of Parliament 1430–31 (9 Hen CX) the provision was made that 'Whoever shall brew ale in the town of Cambridge with the intention of selling it must have a sign otherwise he shall forfeit his ale'. In effect, the sign was the licence to sell liquor, and its removal symbolised the termination of that licence. This set publicans apart from other tradesmen whose signs were optional. While communities were small, street numbers or signs were not needed, but as towns grew, the identification of properties became necessary, and at a time when

Above: Detail from a painting of a roadside inn by George Morland showing a sign complete with its bunch of grapes. Below: The White Hart Inn at Schoale, Norfolk: an 1825 engraving published by T. McLean in 1842.

A much simpler style of sign spanning the road: The Halfway House. A mailcoach outside the Greyhound Inn *by James Pollard.*

literacy and numeracy were by no means general, this had to be done by symbols. Charles I in a Charter to the citizens of London on his accession to the throne in 1625 stated

> that it may and shall be lawful to the citizens of the same city . . . for the time being, to expose and hang in and over the streets and ways and alleys of the said City and suburbs the same signs and posts affixed to their houses and shops, for the better finding out of such citizens' dwellings, shops, arts or occupations.[1]

Thus both private houses and business premises bore signs.

The 'beam' sign which spanned a road gave the greatest scope to the craftsmen, and probably the most elaborate sign ever made was of this type. It was made for the White Hart Inn, Schoale, now Scole, in the seventeenth century and, apart from the white hart itself, was a veritable triumphal arch all carved in wood, including the Roman garlands of evergreen, Jonah emerging from the whale's mouth, Neptune on a dolphin, and Charon carrying a witch to Hades. The whole phantasmagorical composition was surmounted by an astronomer who is 'seated on a circumferenter and by some chymical preparations is so affected that in fine weather he faces that quarter from which it is about to come'. The whole structure disappeared over one hundred years ago but not before it was engraved in 1825 by 'C. J. R.' in a print published by T. McLean in 1842 (a copy is in Norwich Central Library). Although this example was exceptional, other large signs were constructed. M. Grisley, a Frenchman travelling in England in 1765, noted as he landed at Dover:

> I saw nothing remarkable but the enormous size of the public-house signs, the ridiculous magnificence of the ornaments with which they are overcharged, the height of a sort of triumphal arches that support them and most of which cross the streets.[3]

The extravagance of these signs soon developed into a hazard for those passing beneath them. After the Great Fire of London shopkeepers were encouraged to have signs carved in a stone panel let into the face of the building.[4] A number of examples of these are preserved in the Museum of London. However, this type of sign was not so visible and it was not long before the 'gallows' sign re-appeared in London. Such signs helped the stranger find his way about town:

> If drawn by Bus'ness to a Street unknown,
> Let the sworn Porter point thee throgh the town;
> Be sure observe the signs, for signs remain
> Like faithfull landmarks to the walking train.

They could even forecast the weather!

> But when the swinging signs your ears offend
> With creaking noise, then raining floods impend.
> (John Gay)

However, not all writers were so complimentary. An article in Richard Steele's *Tatler* for 20 May 1709 (no. 18) remarks that

> Many a man has lost his way and his dinner by the general want of skill in orthography: for considering that the painters are usually so very bad, that you cannot know the animal under whose sign you are to live that day, how must the stranger be misled if it is wrong spelled, as well as ill-painted?

In spite of the autocratic outlook of those who were disciples of 'high' art, there was in the eighteenth century a sneaking regard for the products of the sign painter and carver. In *The Spectator* for 8 January 1743 may be found the following passage:

> The other day going down Ludgate Street, several people were gaping at a very splendid sign of Queen Elizabeth which far exceeded all other signs in the street, the painter having shewn a masterly judgment, and the carver and gilder much pomp and splendour. It looked rather like a capital picture in a gallery than a sign in a street.

Between about 1625 and 1775 street signs were a successful public art form and visitors from abroad were constantly referring to them. So successful were trade signs that in 1695 the House of Commons proposed to raise 'half a million of money per annum with a great ease to the subject by a tax upon signs'.[5] A Frenchman named Misson, travel-

Stone sign for the pipe works of Joshua Lee, No. 11 Sidney Street, Cambridge.

Hogarth's 1762 engraving The Times, *Plate 1, shows the crowded streets full of signs.*

ling in England in about 1698, wrote that 'at London they [signs] are commonly very large and jut out so far that in some narrow streets they touch one another; nay, and run across almost quite to the other side'. This had the effect of drastically reducing the light in narrow alleys. Such hanging signs also constituted a potential danger to passers by. In 1718 a sign in Bride Lane fell to the ground bringing down the front of a house and killing four people.[6] Legislation prohibiting the use of signs was not forthcoming until such time as an alternative method of identifying property had been devised. In Hatton's *A New View of London* published in 1708 the following description may be found:

> Prescot Street, a spacious and regular built Street on the South side of the Tenter Ground in Goodman's Fields—instead of Signs the houses here are distinguished as the staircases in the Inns of Court and Chancery.

This probably marks one of the earliest uses of street numbering in England.* The numbering of houses was however slow to be accepted and the 1763 *Directory* lists a total of only thirty-one numbered addresses in London, and six of these were for houses in Prescot Street.[7] Larwood and Hotten state that an examination of about two thousand Fire Insurance Policies for the years 1721–27 produced only two examples of a property being identified by a street

number. In 1763 building regulations were introduced in the City of Westminster that affected the use of signs on gallows. The removal of signs in the City of London followed with orders for dismantling:

> All signs or other emblems used to denote the trade, occupation or calling of any person or persons, signposts, signirons, balconies, penthouses, showboards, spouts and gutters projecting into the said streets, etc, and all other encroachments projections and annoyances whatsoever within the said cities and Liberties.[8]

Inns and public houses alone seemed to remain outside this law, no doubt because of earlier Acts of Parliament that made the use of signs mandatory for those selling alcohol. Thenceforth the trade sign was in decline and street numbering became usual, though not without a sense of loss for those bad and decorative 'old days': *

> The Scottish new pavement† well deserves our praise
> To the Scotch too we're obliged to for mending our ways:
> But this we can never forgive for they say
> As that they have taken our posts all away.[1]

As has been seen, the monastic hospice was the predecessor of some inns and their connection with the church or with a college was often denoted by a group of signs of a religious nature such as the Mitre, the Virgin and the Angel. It is possible that even the old favourite, the Bull, is a sign of this class and that it refers to a Papal Bull, such documents from Rome having a seal bearing the device of the bull of St Luke. There were once so many signs of this type that Richard Flecknoe, writing in his *Aenigmatical Characters* (1665), wrote of the effects of the Commonwealth as follows:

> As for the signs, they have pretty well begun their reformation already, changing the sign of the Salutation of our Lady into the Soldier and Citizen and the Catherine Wheel into the Cat and Wheel; such ridiculous work they make of this reformation and so jealous they are against all mirth and jollity, as they would pluck down the Cat and Fiddle too, if it durst but play so loud as they might hear it.

Many signs are not only heraldic in treatment, for it is to the herald also that they owe their inspiration, the arms being those of their owner: prelate, lord or the King himself. It is to the monarchy that we owe the White Swan of Edward III, the Portcullis (also the Harrow) of John of Gaunt, the White Hart of Richard II, the Antelope of Henry IV, the Blue Boar of Richard III, the Falcon of

*Earlier directories do not give numbered addresses, for example, 'A Collection of names of the merchants living in the City of London, printed for Sam Lee and are to be sold at his shop in Lombard Street near Popes-head-Alley: and Dan Major at the Flying Horse in Fleet Street', 1677.

*In Paris, street numbering was general by 1787 and compulsory by 1805.
†Aberdeen granite sets.

Top left: *Sign for The George & Dragon, Norwich, an inn recorded at the beginning of the 19th century.*
Top right: *Carved wooden figure for The White Hart, Bath, Somerset.*
Above left: *This Black Bull could have been either an inn sign or a butcher's shop sign.*
Above right: *Carved figure for The Great White Horse, Ipswich, Suffolk.*

Opposite, top: *The George & Dragon, West Meon, Hampshire and The White Hart, South Harting, both with bunches of grapes.*
Bottom: *Sign for The John Gilpin, Gold Street, Cambridge, painted by Richard Hopkins Leach (1794–1851) and removed in 1910.*

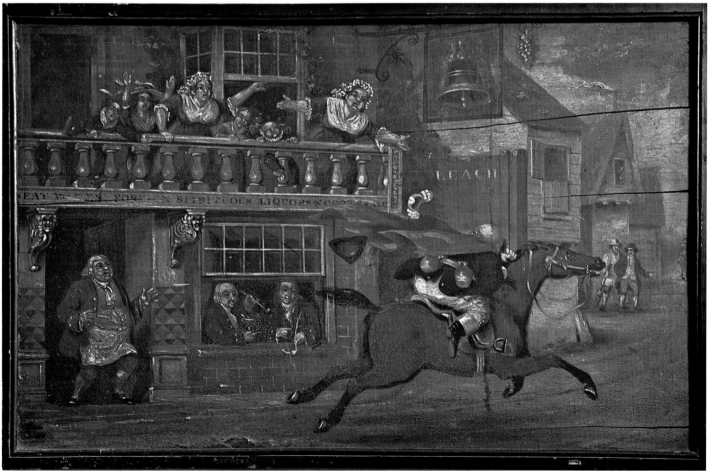

Above: *Carved sign for The Sun Inn, Oak Street, Norwich, probably mid-18th century.*
Opposite, top left: *The Black Swan: a mid-19th century inn sign painted on fir (36in x 48in).* Top right: *The Wheatsheaf, early 19th century inn sign of oak, painted and gilt (34in high), from an inn at 27 Broad Street, Bath.*
Bottom: *The Friesian Bull, a late 19th century sign used for butcher's shops and inns.*

Edward IV, the Greyhound of Henry VII, the White Rose of the Tudors (York), the Red Rose of Lancaster, the Lion of the Stuarts and the White Horse of the House of Hanover. The Crown always denoted loyalty, no matter which dynasty occupied the throne, though the same was not true of the Royal Arms. The Sun or the Rising Sun was not only an emblem of Edward III but also formed an element in the coat of arms of the Distillers' Company. The badges and crests of great families were also adopted, such as the Bear (and ragged staff) of Warwick,* and the Talbot, the hunting dog now extinct which was adopted by the Talbots, Earls of Shrewsbury, as supporters for their coat of arms. Lions of various colours were once popular as inn signs. The Golden Lion refers to the arms of England and the Red Lion of Scotland. The White Lion forms part of

*See Shakespeare's Henry VI in which Warwick swears by 'The rampant bear chained to the ragged staff'. As a crest it must have derived from bear-baiting.

the arms of the Howards, Dukes of Norfolk; the Blue is from the Mildmay arms, while the Black refers to de Crespigny. Howitt[9] in describing rural inns says that

> the travelling carriages stop to bait [=to eat] there, for it is between towns, the squire comes there occasionally, for he patronises it, and has his private and public meetings held there. Most probably it is his own property and its sign the arms of his family; and what is quite likely the landlord is his old servant . . . who [has] . . . *retired* to public life . . . in nine cases out of ten he has a farm attached to his Inn.

In this people's art of the pub sign many less aristocratic references occur, among them *sporting*—the Dog and Duck, the Bat and Ball, etc, *agricultural*—the Hop Pole, the Barley Mow, the Plough, *nautical*—the Anchor, the Ship and *craft*—the Mason's Arms, the Carpenter's Arms.

> There is nothing more characteristic of rural life than a village alehouse or inn. It is the centre of information . . . I do not mean the low pothouse—the new beer-shop of the new Beer-Bill, with LICENSED TO BE DRUNK ON THE PREMISES blazoned over the door in staring characters—the Tom-and-Jerry of the midland counties—the Kidley-Wink of the west of England. No, I mean the good old-fashioned country alehouse, . . . there is the old spreading tree, that is as old, probably older, than the inn itself. It is an elm, with a knotty mass of root swelled out around the base of its sturdy stem into a prodigious heap—into a seat, in fact, on holiday occasions for a score of rustic revellers, or resters. In some cases, . . . a good stout bench runs round it; or where the root is at all endangered by scratching dogs, picking and hewing children, or rooting pigs of the village . . . it is protected by a circle of wattled fence.

You see the tree is a tree of mark and consequence, it is indeed *the tree*. It is looked upon as part and parcel of the concern of as much consequence to the house as its sign; and it is often the sign itself, THE OLD ELM TREE.[9]

Howitt goes on to cite other trees to be found outside the village inn, including the ash and the oak. Reference to yew trees implies the continuing tradition since Roman times for the evergreen in this situation. Sometimes a whole group of trees was planted by the inn and but one tree remains; 'see the sign hangs in it, or is suspended on its post, just by, by bearing the likeness of the original tree *attempted* by some village artist'. He describes 'The Golden Grove, kept by James Snowden' at St Anne's Hill, Chertsey, Surrey. 'There you have the picture of The Golden-Grove all in a blaze of gold—somewhat dashed and dimmed, it is true, by the blaze of many suns,—but there it is, in front of the inn, and by the old tree'.

Shop and Trade Signs

In Ancient Egypt the Pharaoh was portrayed holding the shepherd's crook and the farmer's flail. As a symbol of kingship the use of these trade implements declined, though the crook was used as a crosier, the Bishop's staff of office. Both the flail and the crook continued as the symbols of humble rural callings. Thomas Hardy in *Far from the Madding Crowd* describes the farm labourers standing by the cross on market day waiting for employment with the tools of their trade:

> At one end of the street stood from two to three hundred blithe and hearty labourers waiting upon Chance—all men of the stamp to whom labour suggests nothing worse than a wrestle with gravitation, and pleasure nothing better than a renunciation of the same. Among these, carters and waggoners were distinguished by having a piece of whip-cord twisted round their hats; thatchers wore a fragment of woven straw; shepherds held their sheep crooks in their hands; and thus the situation required was known to the hirers at a glance.

Just as the Bishop transformed the simple crook into a bejewelled and opulent model of the original implement, so in some instances models were made of various trade tools for processional use. The shipwrights of Bristol, for example, made colossal replicas in wood of the axe, the chisel and the mall or beetle. It was perhaps an extension of this practice that led to the use of trade signs.

In *The Complete English Tradesman* (1727) Daniel Defoe makes the following distinction between the tradesman and the shopkeeper:

> In the North of Britain, and likewise in Ireland, when you speak of a tradesman you are understood to mean a mechanic . . . in like manner, abroad they call a tradesman such only as carry goods about . . . from market to market . . . trading men . . . whether wholesale or retail, are grocers, mercers, linen and woollen drapers etc etc . . . On the other hand, those who

Left: trade sign said to have been used to advertise a chimney sweep, made from sheet tin and painted wood (47in high).

Centre and right: Two trade cards from the Ambrose Heal collection, now in the British Museum.

From ỹ Black Spread Eagle in Shandoies Street

GABRIEL DOVCE at ỹ Lamb & Black Spread Eagle next door to the Golden Goate in New Round Court in ỹ Strand. Selleth all Sorts of Silks Stuffs Norwich Crapes Camlells & all sorts of Black Silks for Hoods & Scarves at Reasonable Rates

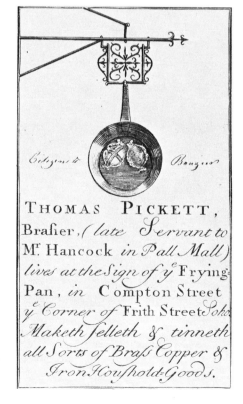

THOMAS PICKETT, Brasier, (late Servant to Mr. Hancock in Pall Mall) lives at the Sign of ỹ Frying Pan, in Compton Street ỹ Corner of Frith Street Soho Maketh Selleth & tinneth all Sorts of Brass Copper & Iron Houshold Goods.

make the goods they sell, tho' they do keep shops to sell them, are not called tradesmen but handicraftsmen, such as smiths, shoemakers, founders, joiners, carpenters, carvers, turners and the like, others who only make, or cause to be made, goods for other people to sell, are called manufacturers and artists, etc . . . As there are several degrees of people employ'd in trade below these, such as workmen, labourers and servants; so there is a degree of traders above them which we call merchants.

As with the distinction between the inn and the public house, the distinction between the shopkeeper and the tradesman was often blurred. The word 'trade' in fact derives from the Old English 'trod', footstep or well trodden path, and it retains this meaning in 'trade wind'.

'Tradesman', 'mechanic' or 'handicraftsman', 'manufacturer' or 'merchant', all in the seventeenth and eighteenth centuries used signs outside their premises. Indeed Defoe is very critical (in Letter XIX) of 'Fine Shops, and Fine Shews' and he concludes that

> . . . the customers, . . . are such as are gain'd by and preserv'd by good usage, good pennyworths, good wares, and good choice; and a shop that has the reputation of these four, like good wine that needs no bush, needs no painting and gilding, no carv'd works and ornaments; it requires only a diligent master and a faithful servant and it will never want a trade.

Few of these 'carv'd works and ornaments' have survived from the seventeenth and eighteenth centuries and it is principally through the work of topographical artists and contemporary trade cards that we know the appearance of many of these signs. These cards have survived in remarkably large numbers, perhaps because they were considered as objects of curiosity in their own time. One of the first collectors was Samuel Pepys, whose collection of Vulgaria is still intact in the Pepysian Library at Magdalene College, Cambridge. In this century Ambrose Heal formed a fine collection, now in the Department of Prints and Drawings in the British Museum; he also published a number of books on the subject. Often these signs attached to the outside of buildings bore some relationship to the activity or commodity available within. However, this was by no means always the case and, as time went by, these emblems became more and more remote from the goods that they were designed to advertise. 'Our streets are filled with Blue Boars, Black Swans and Red Lions not to mention Flying Pigs and Hogs in Armour with other creatures more extraordinary than any in the deserts of Africk', wrote Addison for the 28th number of *The Spectator*, 2 April 1710. He continued '. . . I would enjoin every shop to make use of a

sign which bears some affinity to the wares in which it deals. What can be more inconsistent than to see a bawd at the sign of the Angel or a taylor at the Lion?' Such inconsistency was not uncommon. Consistency, as Addison went on to point out, would require that 'Hence the Hand and Shears is justly appropriate to the Taylors and the Hand and Pen to the Writing masters.' Reference to Ambrose Heal's *The Signboards of Old London Shops* shows that such logic was occasionally to be met with, and he illustrates a trade card for one John Johnson, woollen draper, at the Hand and Shears in Southwark c.1760, while the same writer in his *English Writing Masters and their Copy-Books 1570–1800* (Cambridge University Press 1931) alludes to John Ayres (fl. 1680–1705) as advertising himself in 1680 as 'Master of the Writing School at the "Hand and Pen" near St Paul's School in St Paul's Church Yard'.

There is in fact a group of signs that became very much associated with a particular trade or profession and heraldry was, as with the inn signs, the source of many of these. The three brass balls of the pawnbroker, for example, are said to

Pawnbroker's sign from the shop owned by the late Mr A. Mann, All Saints Green, Norwich. These familiar signs were originally painted blue.

Above left: A carved Golden Fleece, the traditional sign of the woollen draper's trade, from the shop of Elam Skoyles, formerly Riches and Skoyles of Davey Place, Norwich.
Left: Trade card of Richard Fawson, Woollen Draper.
Above: Pawnbroker's shop sign.

be derived from the coat of arms of the Medici, principal among the Lombardy bankers after whom Lombard Street in the City of London is named. It was however the various City Companies that inspired many signs, for example the Cradle of the Basket Makers, the Cupid and Torch of the Glaziers, the Compasses of the Carpenters, the Goat's Heads of the Cordwainers, the Leopards' Heads of the Weavers, the Tents of the Upholders, the Doves of the Tallow-Chandlers, Adam and Eve of the Fruiterers, the Elephant and Castle of the Cutlers, the Maiden-head of the Mercers, the Rasp of the Snuff-makers, the Cup of the Goldsmiths, the Teazle of the Clothworkers and the Green Man, the supporter of the arms of the Distillers.

Professional men invariably made reference to the learned, hence booksellers had signs made in the form of heads of literary men, thus the Shakespeare's Head, or Virgil's, or Pope's. Scientific instrument makers likewise used heads of Tycho Brahé, Archimedes, Sir Isaac Newton and others, with the chemists and apothecaries using the Galen, the Glauber and the Boerhaave Head, while artists' colourmen and print-sellers took the Rembrandt or the Hogarth Head as their sign.

Patron saints of various occupations were also adopted: St Crispin and St Hugh for shoemakers, St Luke for the painters' colourmen, St Peter and his keys for the locksmiths, and St Lawrence and his gridiron, or St Dunstan with his pincers, for the smiths. In addition to or in place of the sign of St Hugh, the shoemaker might have the sign of the Golden Boot, as the grocer would have the Sugar Loaf, the cabinet-maker the Walnut Tree, the chemist the Pestle and Mortar and the dairy the Cow's Head.

Effigies of monarchs made popular signs, among them Henry VIII, Elizabeth I and Charles II or his 'Royal Oak'; the Royal Arms were also adopted. Grinling Gibbons, as Master Carver in Wood to the Crown (Charles II to George I), lived at the sign of the King's Arms in Bow Street from 1687 to his death in 1721.[10]

The introduction of tobacco to England coincides with the rise in the importance of trade signs following the Royal Charter of 1625, which permitted the use of signs in London. No doubt some early traders in tobacco took for a sign a carved or painted head of the man who was often held responsible for the introduction of the weed. The following is a letter printed in *The General Advertiser* on 13 March 1784:

Sir,—Being a smoker, I take particular notice of the devices used by different dealers in tobacco, by way of ornament to the papers in which that valuable plant is enclosed for sale; and that used by the worthy Aldermen in Ludgate Street, has often given me much pleasure, it having the head of Sir Walter Raleigh, and the following motto round it:

"Great Britain to great Raleigh owes
This plant and country where it grows"

To which I offer the following lines by way of contrast; the truth thereof no one can doubt:

"To Rubicon and North, old England owes
The loss of country where tobacco grows."

I suppose no dealer will chuse to adopt so unfortunate a subject for their insignia, but perhaps, when you have a spare corner in your *General Advertiser*, it may not be inadmissible, which will oblige—Yours etc.

A. Smoker.

Raleigh's head does not seem to have been widely adopted, perhaps because James I had removed it—a mark of disapproval of lasting consequences. There were, however, four signs used by tobacconists, and these were perennially popular. The Blackamoor, the Tobacco Roll, the Highlander, and the Snuff Rasp. The Turk was also occasionally used.

Left: The Golden Boot above a boot-maker's shop in Bath.
Centre: Trade card showing the sugar loaves of the grocer.

Right: Carved wooden figure of a Turk from Bacon's Tobacco Shop, Market Hill, Cambridge.

The 'Black Boy' sign of carved wood had in the late seventeenth century a cherubic character fashionable at the time, in contrast to the more adult proportions of the Blackamoor of a century later. In both instances the figure is shown wearing a 'kilt' and head-dress of conventionalised multicoloured tobacco-leaves which produce a feathered effect, as much as to suggest 'America' by reference to her aborigines. No doubt this is how such signs were interpreted by Americans visiting Europe.* Indian Queens, Indian Chiefs and Indian Kings were all popular in England as inn signs after the visit of four Iroquois 'Kings' to England in 1710.

Tobacconists apparently used the sign of the Black Boy from the first, for in Ben Jonson's *Bartholomew Fair* (Act 1,

*The Blackamoor was also used as a sign by tobacconists in Holland and France.

Left: *Black Boy figure c1720.* Below, left: *18th century Blackamoor figure from the shop of Newbegin, Bridewell Alley, Norwich. The figure has a roll of tobacco under the left arm and a snuff horn in the right hand.* Centre: *Nubian figure c1780 with a roll of tobacco under the arm.* Right: *Tobacconist's figure of a Moor, c1830.*

Scene 1) is the following line: 'I thought he would have run mad o' the Black Boy in Bucklersbury, that takes the scurvy roguy tobacco there'. The Tobacco Roll does not often seem to have been used as a sign on its own, though it was often used in association with the figure of a black boy. At other times tobacco rolls were used in groups, for example, 'Felton at ye Three Tobacco Rolls, in Long Acre', (c. 1750).[11] Another symbol employed by the tobacconist was the snuff rasp, and reference to signs such as the Rasp and Crown are often to be found.[11] Many shopkeepers ignored the conventions of their trade and used utterly unrelated signs. One such was 'John Hardham at the Red Lyon in Fleet Street', though in this instance the sign might well refer to Scotland. Hardham, a friend of David Garrick, was well known for his 'No. 37' snuff.

After the Act of Union between England and Scotland in 1707, Glasgow become one of the chief ports for the importation of American tobacco and the carved wooden

Below: Tobacconist's sign of two rolls of tobacco painted gold and black. Right: Front and back views of carved wooden Highlanders.

figure of a Highlander, often holding a snuff-mull and proffering a pinch of snuff, became a popular sign for tobacconists. (The sculptor Nollekens, a regular snuff taker, 'preferred rapee' but 'he would put up with an early pinch of Scotch from a North Briton'.[12]) However, there is another more romantic explanation for the Sign of the Highlander on such premises. 'David Wishart (at ye Highlander, Thistle and Crown at ye upper end of St James', Hay Market, in Coventry Street)'[11] was, in about 1720, one of the first to use the figure of a Highlander, and it is in fact thought that he originated the custom. In his case the figure indicated a Jacobite rendezvous.

Many of the figures of the sort used by tobacconists and others are small in scale and clearly not designed to be exhibited out of doors. Furthermore many such wood-carvings are elaborately finished at the back and were thus designed to be seen in the round as an emblem of the trade inside the shop.

By a statute still in force [1797] the barbers and surgeons were each to use a pole as a sign. The barbers were to have their's blue and white striped, and with no further appendage, but the surgeons [which were

the same in other respects] were to have a gallipot and a red flag in addition to denote the particular nature of their vocation.[13]

This derives from the time when barbers practised phlebotomy. The patient grasped a pole to make the blood flow more freely and this became covered with blood and barbers are said to have twisted linen bandages round the pole to produce the familiar barber pole which they hung outside their houses. [The addition of a blue stripe was often made in the painted sign but without any particular reason.] Larwood and Hotten[14] quote but do not attribute the following description in verse:

His pole with pewter basons hung,
Black, rotten teeth in order strung,
Rang'd cups that in a window stood
Lined with red rags to look like blood,
Did well his threefold trade explain,
Who shave, drew teeth, and breathed a rein.

Barbers, in common with others, do not seem to have confined themselves to a pole to signal their premises, if Hogarth's 'Night' is to be trusted:

The last plate, is a description of NIGHT, and that, a rejoicing one, viz. the 29th May; evident from the bonfires, the oaken bough upon the barbers pole, and the oak leaves some have fixed in their hats. The scene is taken from the narrow part of Charing-Cross . . . exhibits to view the Rummer tavern on one side, and, the Cardigan's head on the other; at the time two noted bagnios . . . on the right . . . is the house of a barber-surgeon, illuminated with candles, whose sign is, a hand, drawing a tooth; the head in exquisite pain, beneath is written "shaving, bleeding, and teeth drawn with a touch. ECCE SIGNUM".[15]

Though many signs were in use that directly referred to the trade concerned through the use of tools or materials as emblems, and though others referred to the trade in a more obscure way through, for example, the arms of a City Company, an equal and perhaps greater number of premises were identified in an apparently arbitrary way. A 'species' of premises was, as we have seen, frequently identified by the use of a particular device, for example, the bush or bunch of grapes of the inn or the red and white pole of the barber. However, this did nothing to identify an individual innkeeper or barber. This provided the cue for what might be termed the double-barrelled sign, one half signifying the 'generic' character of the business, the other half the particular concern. Of course many double-barrelled signs were inevitable due to the nature of the subject, for example, The Hand and Glove. It was the secondary part of the title that often gave rise to confusion. This was caused

by a shopkeeper continuing to use the sign of the business previously occupying the shop, coupled with an emblem of his own. Addison, writing in *The Spectator* (2 April 1710, No. 28), referred to another related practice as follows:

I must however observe to you upon this subject that it is usual for a young tradesman on his first setting up to add his own sign to that of the master whom he served, as the husband after marriage gives place to his mistress's arms in his own coat.

Below: *Engraving of Hogarth's painting* Night
Right: *Bristol Shipwrights' Company processional axe of carved and painted wood, with representations of Noah's Ark on both sides of the 3ft 6in long blade. Early 19th century.*
Below right: *A group of signs referring directly to a trade by showing either its tools or its product: the sign of The Golden Glove from S. & H. Webb, Outfitters of 3/5 Dove Street, Norwich; The Golden Plane of H. Griffiths & Son, formerly of 26 Lower Goat Lane, Norwich. Griffiths were planemakers and tool dealers from the early part of the 19th century; The Padlock and Key of P. G. Fountain Ltd., Builder's Ironmongers, 31 Pottergate, Norwich.*

NIGHT.

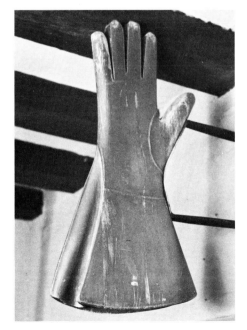

The Makers of Signs

The signs that survive on medieval inns form an integral part of the original structure of the building, as for example the angel in carved stone which supports the oriel window of the inn of that name at Grantham, Lincolnshire. It may therefore be inferred that such signs were made as part of the stock-in-trade of the architectural stone-carver and in medieval times little or nothing separated the character of work found on temporal or ecclesiastical property, neither was there a parallel distinction between 'high art' and 'folk art'. This position no doubt continued for a hundred years or so after the dissolution of the monasteries. One of the earliest of these post-Reformation signs was found buried in a mound of rubbish at Whitechapel, brought there after the Great Fire. It represented a carved boxwood boar's head in a circular frame formed by two boar's tusks united with silver. The carving was inscribed 'Wm Brooke, Landlord of the *Bore's Hedde, Eastchepe* 1566'. This sign, which in view of its materials was designed for display indoors, was once in the collection of the publisher Stamford. It was sold at Christies on 27 January 1855 to a Mr Halliwell; shortly afterwards a line drawing appeared in the *Illustrated London News* (p. 181, 24th February, 1855).

Signs of a type that would be recognised today do not seem to have entered the street scene much before the seventeenth century. As has been seen, signs were used to identify business premises and private houses although the latter often, and the inn sometimes, favoured the expedient of giving an address, as 'At The Blue Door', or 'The Red House'. In Dean Street, Soho, London, there was a house identified by 'Two Blue Flower Pots', and in Great Gardens, Bristol, another house known simply as 'The Brass Knocker';[16] Caxton's 'Red Pole', signifying his printing shop, was an extension of this idea.

Common though signs once were in England in the seventeenth and eighteenth centuries, very few surviving

Previous pages
Left: *The Bricklayer's Arms, oil on fir panel from the early 19th century, 17in x 41½in.*
Centre: *A Highlander advertising snuff and tobacco, carved and painted wood, 37in high, early 19th century.*
Right: *Mid-18th century tobacconist's Blackamoor sign, carved and painted wood, 32in x 11in x 15in.*
Opposite, Above: *Shop sign in painted wood used to advertise snuff and tobacco.*
Below: *Carved stone sign set into the building of The Swan Inn, Clare, Suffolk.*

18th century wrought iron sign bracket from The Fox Inn, Huntingdon.

examples date back so far. Lacking a comprehensive body of specimens to study for their internal evidence, we are compelled to look at contemporary references in topographical views, written accounts, street directories, trade cards and even trade tokens.[17] The token coinage of the nineteenth century is of some interest, but it is from earlier specimens that most information may be derived and these date mostly from between 1648–1679.

It appears that at some point in the seventeenth century street sign-makers became a specialised branch of the crafts of wood-carving and painting, though it is likely that the supporting brackets for signs continued to be made by general smiths. In London most of these sign-makers were concentrated in Harp Alley, Shoe Lane:

> . . . where until lately, gilt grapes, sugar loaves, lasts, teapots, etc., etc. were exposed ready for market. Here Messrs Barlow, Craddock, and others whose names are now as completely lost as their works, had studios, and produced very creditable signs both carved and painted.[18]

The diversity of work undertaken by such artists is revealed by some surviving trade cards, for example that of 'Willi Steward (at the) King's Head in Fleet Street'[19], who:

> Selleth signes ready painted and Bushes for Taverns, Border Cloths for shops, Constables Staffes, Laurells for Clubs, Dyall Boards for Clocks, Sugar Loaves and Tobacco-roles.

41

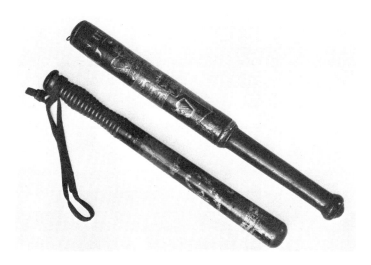

As few early signs have survived, it is helpful to know that the same artists made 'Constables Staffes' which have survived in considerable numbers and that 'Dyall Boards for Clocks' were considered as a related art. This diversity was not exceptional. Thomas Proctor's trade card of circa 1730 states that he 'Selleth all sorts of signs, Bushes, Bacchus's, Bunches of Grapes and Show Boards at Reasonable Prices'.

It is possible that Mr Bradford, Mr Demancing, John Demanel and Mr Richmond, who are all listed as living in Harp Lane in *A Collection of the Names of the Merchants Living in and about the City of London* (1677), were also shop sign-makers although the only signs mentioned in the street directory are those of 'The Goldsmiths that keep Running Cashes', in other words, the bankers of the seventeenth century. To the known sign-makers, Barlow, Craddock, Steward and Proctor, not a single work may be assigned.

In *Hogarth Moralized* published in 1767 'with the Approbation of Jane Hogarth' there appears a lengthy description of *Beer Street*. This print shows a sign-board artist at work *in situ*; maintenance must have been a significant part of the Harp Alley businesses:

> Though Mr Hogarth has thought proper in print to show the advantage almost every individual receives from drinking this valuable liquor [beer] which is at so low a price, as to be within the compass of a poor man's pocket; yet, he has given us a painter (painting a sign, viz. The Barley Mow) in all the appearance of want, though happy, and, smiling under it. Whether he intended the leaness, and tattered condition of this man as a contrast to the corpulent, tight dressed figures of the men below, or, whether, by lowering his own profession, while he raises those of others, is im-

Left: *The Golden Teapot, sign of Robert Fox, grocer and tea dealer of St Saviour's Lane, Norwich; the sign was transferred to the grocery of John Dodson in Magdalen Street in the 1880s.*
Above: *Two painted 'Constables staffes' or truncheons, one dated 1811 from the reign of George III, the other marked 'VR Police' with the name of the maker, Parker, 233 Holborn, inscribed on it.*

> material, let it suffice to say it completes the group, by making it pyramidical; . . . thus it pleases the eye, and perfects the piece . . .

The phrase 'Mr Hogarth has thought proper in print to . . .' etc. is interesting, as the original drawing for this work, now in the Pierpont Morgan Library, had shown a corpulent sign-painter enjoying the delights of beer with other bibulous workers. There is no suggestion in the description of the print of the sign-painter being in anyway inferior to easel painters though it does appear that perhaps this particular sign-painter was not only sober (the bottle hanging from the sign presumably contains an oil medium) but unsuccessful.

That artists of consequence in the 'Polite Arts' produced inn signs there is no doubt. John Thomas Smith published his *Nollekens and his Times* in 1829. Though this is a scurrilous attack by Smith on the man to whom he was apprenticed, it is nevertheless an extremely useful book that throws much light not only on the sculptor but on other eighteenth-century British artists, their views and their lives.* Among the artists that Smith mentions as having painted inn signs was George Morland who 'painted a sign of a White Lion for a public house at Paddington'

*Smith, himself a sculptor, was also at one time Keeper of the Department of Prints and Drawings at the British Museum.

BEER STREET

The engraving of Hogarth's Beer Street, *published in 1751, and his original drawing of the same scene.*

which was much frequented by drovers whose manners Morland appreciated and whose cattle he painted. Hassell's *Life of Morland* mentions a black bull which he painted for an inn on the London to Deal road, and he is also known to have painted a sign for the Goat in Boots, in Fulham Road, and the Cricketers, near Chelsea Bridge, both in London.

Among other artists mentioned in this context by Smith are Zoffany, who painted clock-dials, and, most notably, Clarkson:

> Clarkson, the portrait-painter, was originally a coach panel and sign-painter; and he executed a most elaborate one of Shakespeare which formerly hung across the street at the north-east corner of Little Russell Street [now Russell Street, since 1859] in Drury Lane, the late Mr Thomas Grignon (the watch-maker and jeweller) informed me that he had often heard his father say, that this sign cost five hundred pounds! In my boyish days it was for many years

exposed for sale for a very trifling sum, at a broker's-shop in Lower Brook-street, Grosvenor Square. The late Mr Crace of Great Queen Street,* assured me that it was in his early days a thing that country people would stand and gaze at, and that the corner of the street was hardly passable. Edwards has erroneously given [Samuel] Wale† the credit of this sign.

Whatever the truth as to authorship, Edward Edwards does describe the sign more fully than Smith, adding that it was

> . . . a whole length of Shakespeare, about 5 feet high . . . enclosed in a most sumptious carved gilt frame, and suspended by rich iron work; but this splendid object of attraction did not hang long before it was taken down, in consequence of the Act of Parliament which passed for paving, and also for removing signs and other obstructions in the streets of London. Such was the total change of fashion, and the consequent disuse of signs, that the above represen-

*John Crace, father of Frederick Crace, whose collection of London maps and views is now in the Crace Collection of the British Museum.
†Samuel Wale RA is mentioned by Larwood and Hotten as having painted a sign of Falstaff.

tation of our great dramatic poet was sold for a trifle, to Mason the broker, in Lower Grosvenor-street, where it stood at his door for several years, until it was totally destroyed by the weather and other accidents.[20]

In *Odds and Ends about Covent Garden* by John Green, Wale is again credited with the sign but says that he received 'nearly £200' for it. Daniel Defoe had spoken in *The Complete English Tradesman* (1727) with some criticism of the great expense to which some tradesmen went in setting up shops, adding that 'the Joiners and Painters, Glasiers and Carvers, must have all ready money; the Weavers and Merchants may give credit . . .' Certainly in some prints by Hogarth, for example *The March to Finchley*, signs are shown with very elaborate carved wood frames, though I regret I know of no surviving examples. The great expense of producing such elaborate signs was mentioned by a number of foreign visitors to Britain in the seventeenth and eighteenth centuries including the Frenchman Misson, who, writing in about 1698 of English inn signs, observed that:

> They are generally adorned with carving and gilding, and there are several that with the branches of iron which support them, cost above a hundred guineas.* They seldom write upon the sign the name of the thing represented in it. This does not at all please the German and other travelling strangers; because for want of the things being so named they have not an opportunity of learning their names in England as they stroll along the streets. Out of London and particularly in the villages the signs of inns are suspended in the middle of a great wooden portal, which may be looked upon as a kind of triumphal arch to the honour of Bacchus.

Among the many artists of renown quoted by J. T. Smith as doing this type of work are Charles Catton RA, 1728–98, 'in early life a coach and sign painter' who was known to have produced 'a lion as a sign for his friend Wright, the famous coach-maker'; John Baker RA, 1736–71, 'a famous Flower-painter, decorated coach-panels with borders and wreaths of flowers' and 'Richard Wilson the landscape-painter once condescended to paint a sign of the 'Three Loggerheads' for the house so called, near the spot where he died†. Peter Monamy the marine painter painted a sign for the Porto Bello near the church in St Martin's Lane and also decorated a carriage for Admiral Byng.

Many of the signs which owned their origin to heraldic devices must have been influenced by the heraldic painters.

*Significantly the price is quoted in guineas as for professional rather than commercial services.

†The alehouse was at Llanberis, near Mold, North Wales.

A spectacular heraldic trade sign displayed for many years by Mr Harry Broughton, fishmonger, of 39 St Stephen's Street, Norwich. In 1534 the Stock and Salt Fishmongers Ancient companies combined and their arms were united on a single shield.

J. T. Smith singles out 'Mr Smith, the celebrated artist, who served his time under a Herald-painter of the name of Bromley . . .'

Artists not mentioned by Smith but listed by Larwood and Hotten include Ibbetson as the author of a sign for an alehouse at Troutbeck, Ambleside; David Cox for his work for the Royal Oak at Bettws-y-Coed, Caernarvon; the elder Crome for his sign of the Sawyers at St Martins, Norwich; Sir Charles Ross for the sign of the Magpie at Sudbury; Herring for the Flying Dutchman at Cottage Green, Camberwell, London, and the White Lion at Doncaster; and Millais' George and Dragon for Vidler's Inn, Hays, Kent. Apparently Harlow painted a sign with the front and back views of Queen Charlotte as a pastiche of the work of Sir Thomas Lawrence which Harlow initialled 'T.L.'!

In addition to the artists who made sign-boards as an excursion from their usual run of work, Edwards[20] adds the names of others besides the 'great professors' such as Lamb, Gwyne, Thomas Wright of Liverpool, Ralph Kirby (drawing master to George III) and Robert Dalton (keeper of pictures for George III). The making of signs in the nineteenth century became a matter for the various trade manuals that became so popular at that time. Nathaniel Whittock's advice in *The Painters' and Glaziers' Guide* (London 1827) remains valid to this day. In Chapter X *Sign Painting, Lettering etc.* Whittock remarks that

> The fault that sign painters most easily fall into is that of attempting subjects too difficult to perform, and which, when executed, are too complicated for a sign

Above: *This painted sign was attached to the letter box of William Haddon Smith, Newsagent and Bookseller of 7 Rose Crescent, Cambridge. Into the box were put communications to* The Gownsman, *a university magazine which ran to 17 issues in 1829 and 1830.*

Right: *Inn sign for* The Man Loaded with Mischief *painted by Richard Hopkins Leach of Cambridge. This is a copy of an original sign painted by Hogarth for the inn of the same name in Oxford Street, London.*

board. Signs should only have a single figure (unless it is a compound sign, such as the hare and hounds, etc.) This should be strongly marked, and put in strong light and shade, according to the distance at which it is to be seen; all objects around it should be unobtrusive and as simple as possible. Nothing should attract observation but the principle figure. There are few sign painters can devote any great length of time to the study of the human figure, or animals, from nature; it will in general, therefore, be much better, in subjects where figures are required, for them to copy the works of different artists who have become eminent in their profession, rather than to trust to their own designs.

It appears that Whittock regarded lettering as falling outside the scope of the 'decorative painter' but with some apology he devotes part of the same chapter to the subject. At such an early date (pub. 1827) it is worthy of note that he refers to 'the projecting letters, formed of wood or metal, [that] have of late become so fashionable that the writers on shop fronts, sign boards, etc. have had recourse to imitating them. . . .' Such lettering became the height of fashion in the late nineteenth century.

Artists of all levels of self and public esteem painted signs, but of the names that have come down to us most have been recorded for their importance as easel painters, and almost no examples of their sign painting have survived. Hogarth is an exception, and it was he who assisted Bonnell

Thornton with the 'Grand Exhibition* [of] The Society of Sign Painters', announced in the St James Chronicle of Tuesday 23 March, 1762, as 'a most magnificent Collection of Portraits, Landscapes, Fancy Pieces, Flower Pieces, Night Pieces, Sea Pieces, Sculpture Pieces, etc., etc., designed by the ablest masters and executed by the best hands in the kingdom. Displayed prominently in the exhibition was the following phrase from Horace: SPECTATUM ADMISSI RISUM TENEATIS—You who are let in to look restrain your laughter.† Unfortunately the catalogue produced for this exhibition was something of a burlesque and lists many artists under pseudonyms, including 'Hagarty' for Hogarth. A typical catalogue entry reads:

> 10. A Barge, in Still Life. By Van de Trout. (He cannot properly be called an English artist; not being sufficiently encouraged in his own country, he left Holland with William the Third and was the first artist who settled in Harp Alley).

Or again:

> The Ghost of Cock Lane. By Miss Fanny —. (The figure of two hands, one bearing a hammer, the other a curry comb, an allusion to knocking and scratching).

One catalogue entry in particular, published in the London Register, revealed prevailing attitudes to the visual arts:

> 61. The Robin Hood Society, a Conversation; or Lectures on Elocution. Its Companion. These Two by Barnsley. (These two Strokes at a famous Lecturer on Elocution [No doubt Healey, the orator], and the Reverend Projector of a Rhetorical Academy, are admirably conceived and executed: and (the latter more especially) almost worthy of the Hand of Hogarth. They are full of Variety of droll Figures, and seem to be the Work of a great Master, struggling to suppress his Superiority of Genius, and endeavouring to paint down to the common State and Manner of the School of Sign-painting.)

In the catalogue for this exhibition was the following entry:

> 49. An Ha! Ha!
> 50. (On a parallel Line with the foregoing on the other Side of the Chimney) The Curiosity, its Companion. (These two by an unknown Hand, the Exhibitors being favoured with them from an unknown Quarter.) Ladies and Gentlemen are requested not to finger them, as blue Curtains are hung over in purpose to preserve them. (Behind the blue Curtains on one of these Boards is written Ha! Ha! Ha! and on the other He! He! He! At the first opening of the Exhibition the Ladies had infinite Curiosity to know

what was behind the Curtain, but were afraid to gratify it. This covered Laugh is no bad satire on the indecent Pictures in some Collections, hung up in the same Manner with Curtains over them.)

The exhibition was widely reviewed, although the reviewers occasionally reveal some uncertainty of the real intention of the exhibition. The London Register is clearly referring to Hogarth in the observation that 'To an Artist of our own Times, we owe the Practice of enriching Pictures with Humour'. But how could the eighteenth century be expected to take seriously an exhibition of sign-boards?

> To exercise his [Thornton's] Wit and Humour in an innocent Laugh, and to raise that innocent Laugh in others, seems to have been his chief Aim in the present spectical.

There is some uncertainty in that last sentence, which later gives way to a straightforward description of the exhibits to be found:

> On entering the Grand Room you find yourself in a large and commodious Apartment, hung round with green Bays, on which this curious collection of Wooden Originals is fixt flat, (like the signs at present in Paris) and from whence hang Keys, Bells, Swords, Poles, Sugar-Loaves, Tobacco-Rolls, Candles, and other ornamental Furniture, carved in Wood, that commonly dangle from Penthouses of the different shops in our streets.

The allusion to Paris refers to the results of a by-law there which had ordered that for reasons of safety signs should no longer project into the street but should be fixed flat against walls. It was with Thornton's exhibition of 1762 that the art of the shop sign and the place of their artists reached a high level of fame if not notoriety in Britain, but it was in that same year that the City of London

A pair of carved wooden fish from a fishmonger's shop in Dorchester, Dorset.

ordered the removal of signs within the Square Mile:

> Before this change took place, the universal use of signs furnished no little employment for the inferior rank of painters, and sometimes even the superior professors. Mr Catton painted several very good ones: But, among the most celebrated practitioners in this branch was a person of the name Lamb who possessed a considerable degree of ability: His pencil was bold and masterly, well adapted to the subjects on which it was generally employed. At that time there was a market for signs ready prepared in Harp Alley, Shoe Lane.[20]

Weathervanes

One type of sign not so far considered is the weathervane. Churches were usually surmounted by a cockerel but sometimes, as at St John's, Great Yarmouth, by a fish. On secular buildings, however, a great variety of fish, flesh and fowl were represented.

Both the farmer and the sailor were, and remain, dependent upon the weather. In the pre-technological world one of the few meteorological instruments was the weathervane

18th century cockerel weathervane in repoussé copper (15in x 16in), and copper lion weathervane, early 19th century (5½in x 18½in).

or weathercock (which, significantly, is not known as wind-vane). Such vanes were often created by men with a simple vision whose work may be seen on the grandest of buildings, though it is known that Inigo Jones and Wren also designed them.[21] The vane itself was usually of gilded beaten sheet copper with the cardinal points indicated in wrought iron. These were, in addition to sign brackets, yet another expression of the blacksmith's art. On churches the cardinal points are often omitted as the church itself is orientated. Sometimes weathervanes were made of other materials, such as the gilded fish over St Andrew's Church at Charmouth, Dorset, the body of which is of wood, with fins, teeth and tail of metal. Although ships were commonly used on weathervanes in the Low Countries, few examples survive in Britain. Rochester Town Hall is surmounted by a particularly fine model of Sir Cloudesley Shovell's frigate, *The Rodney,* specially commissioned by the Town Council as a memorial to Shovell. However neither this specimen nor a similar vane in Portsmouth, presented by Prince George of Denmark in 1710, may be considered folk art. Some town hall vanes depict rebuses on the name of the town: Camelford in Cornwall, for example, with its fine embossed copper camel. At other times the vane was used to symbolise the function of the building it surmounted. In Norwich the premises of Moses Levine, a nineteenth-century tobacconist, bore a weathervane in the form of a pipe, while the Nelson Barracks in the same town has a device in the form of a cannon.[22] In London, Billingsgate Fishmarket proudly displays two dolphin vanes (disregarding

zoology) and Leadenhall Market provides a perch for a brace of brazen pheasants. Heraldic vanes were also used, such as the eleven-foot grasshopper, based on the arms of Sir Thomas Gresham, that surmounts the Royal Exchange.

Weathervanes date back to classical antiquity, one of the best known being that which topped the Tower of the Winds in Athens, c. 48 BC. The Bayeux Tapestry illustrates the weathercock that adorned the first Westminster Abbey, but the earliest actual examples to survive in northern Europe are the vanes or pennants of metal from Viking ships. The word 'vane' derives from the Danish *fane* and German *Fahne*, or small flag, which many resemble. In the seventeenth century and before, pennant vanes pierced with a date were common on domestic buildings and these survive *in situ* in large numbers. The earliest dated vane in Norwich is on the church of St John de Sepulchre and has a pierced design including the word *pax* followed by the date 1713, commemorating the Peace of Utrecht.

In the late seventeenth century it was fashionable to connect a weathervane to a dial on a ceiling or wall within a house. An early reference to this 'conceit' occurs in John White's *A Rich Cabinet with a Variety of Inventions*, published in 1651:

> *Receit LVII How to know precisely on the Seeling of a Chamber, which way the wind blowes at all times.*
> This conceit did I see in King James, his Bed chamber in Whitehall: the chamber was an upper Room, having a Vaine or Weather-cock of iron placed above the top or tyles of the house which had a long stem of iron, which did reach thence through the Seeling of the Chamber; upon which Seeling was painted a Marriners compasse . . . Now the lower end of the stem of the Vaine came through the Centre of the compasse, into which was fastened an index or needle (like those in an ordinary Dyall) which doth presently shew how the various wind doth shift from place to place, which you may continually know precisely both night and day.

The size of a weathervane was a major consideration, for it was often placed at a considerable height where, isolated against the sky, the light could diminish its apparent size. This was a problem that Sir Christopher Wren answered empirically. His records show that he employed

> Edward Pearce, mason, for the carving of a wooden dragon, for a modell for ye steeple, and for cutting a

relive in board to be proffered up to discern the right bigness, the sum of £4.

A craftsman in metal was employed to make the final vane. 'To Robert Bird, coppersmith, £38 for making the dragon.' The ultimate horizontal dimension of this beast was nine feet long.

1 Jacob Larwood and John Camden Hotten, *The History of Signboards*, 1866. Jacob Larwood was the English pseudonym of a Dutch writer, Hermann Diederik Johan von Schevichayen, 1827–1918; see *The Signboards of Old London Shops* by Ambrose Heal, London 1947, page 13. Larwood wrote a number of 'Anecdotes', including *A Book of Clerical Anecdotes, Forensic Anecdotes* and *Theatrical Anecdotes*. He also wrote *The Story of the London Parks*.
2 *Encyclopaedia Britannica*, 11th ed, 1910.
3 Albert E. Richardson, *Old Inns of England*, Batsford, London, 1925.
4 Ambrose Heal, *London Tradesmen's Cards of the XVIII Century*, London, 1925, chapter III.
5 Quoted Larwood and Hotten (see 1 above)—Preface VI.
5 Larwood and Hotten (see 1 above), page 26.
6 Quoted by Ambrose Heal in *The Signboards of Old London Shops* (see 1 above).
7 *A Complete Guide to all persons who have any trade or concern in the City of London and parts adjacent*, 1765. The 1768 edition shows a great increase in the numbering of houses and the 1770 edition shows that three-quarters of the premises listed were numerically identified.
8 *Minute Book of the Commissioners of the Parish of Westminster*, 17 May 1763.
9 William Howitt, *Rural Life of England*, 1840.
10 Larwood and Hotten (see 1 above), page 106. 'On Thursday, the house of Mr Gibbons the carver in Bow Street, fell down, but by special providence none of the family were killed'. *Postman* 24 June 1701-2.
11 Ambrose Heal (see 1 above), page 168.
12 J. T. Smith, *Nollekens and his Times*, 1919 ed.
13 Lord Thurlow in the House of Peers, 17 July 1797, quoted by Larwood and Hotten (see 1 above), page 342.
14 Larwood and Hotten (see 1 above), page 342.
15 *Hogarth Moralized*, London, 1767.
16 Larwood and Hotten (see 1 above), page 373.
17 G. C. Williamson, *Trade Tokens*, 1889.
18 Larwood and Hotten (see 1 above), page 37.
19 Ambrose Heal (see 1 above).
20 Edward Edwards, *Anecdotes of Painters*, London, 1808.
21 Margaret Lambert and Enid Marx, *English Popular Art*, London, 1951, see page 29.
22 For further reading see C. J. W. Messent, *The Weathervanes of Norfolk*.

Opposite
Above, left: *An 18th century pennant weathervane.*
Centre and right: *Two engravings illustrating repairs at Ashbourne Church, Derbyshire in 1873; 'Fixing the*

weathervane' and 'The vicar ascending the steeple'.
Below: *Travellers: a Reading caravan built for gypsies c1900 but used by showmen travelling with fairs and circuses.*

The Travellers

Many people lived an itinerant life, but of them it was the Gypsy or Romany who captured the imagination to the extent that many erroneously considered all these travellers to be gypsies. In fact, although Gypsies were often present at fairs and circuses, they did not originally run them. This was the responsibility of the showmen who, while sharing with the Gypsy the itinerant's life, was seldom, if ever, Gypsy by race. 'Lord' George Sanger (1827–1911) makes this quite clear in his autobiography:

> I want to correct here a very popular error—namely the belief that in those early days the gipsies were showmen, and most of the showmen gipsies . . . The showmen proper always kept themselves apart from the gipsies, who invariably camped in a different spot to that occupied by the caravans. I do not think I ever saw genuine gipsies acting as showmen, though I have known them as proprietors of large drinking and dancing booths.[1]

The true Romany was no less certain on this point. When Edward Harvey ('Jon Jinnepen') offered to repaint Ambrose Mill's 'vardo' (waggon) to match the elaborate decoration on the bearer rail, Mill replied 'What do you think I am— a ruddy circus?'[2]

The Romany belongs to a race of which the origin is obscure. Being set apart from the 'host' population by race and way of life, he flourished in Britain particularly when the roads were improved in the nineteenth century. The 'house on wheels' as it was known did not evolve until that time, and Howitt in his chapter on *Gipsies*[3] makes no reference to Gypsy caravans. Until about 1850 Gypsies lived either in tents or in simple shelters constructed of brushwood. It seems that the first travellers to live in caravans were in fact the showmen. An advertisement for Polito's touring menagerie of 1805 describes 'the largest travelling collection in the known world, to be seen in six safe and commodious caravans, built for the purpose'. Caravans built for human occupation were the next logical step. In fact the earliest caravans according to 'Lord' George Sanger were made by the showmen themselves, probably on drays built by cartwrights. Sanger's father was invalided out of Nelson's navy after Trafalgar and became a successful peepshow proprietor. His son described the first home-made caravan as being so hot in summer and so cold in winter that the family continued to live in tents. One of the earliest descriptions of such a vehicle occupied by a travelling waxwork show-woman, Mrs Jarley, occurs in Dickens' *The Old Curiosity Shop* (1840):

> It was not a shabby, dingy, dusty cart, but a smart little house upon wheels, with white dimity curtains festooning the windows, and window-shutters of green

Opposite: *A Burton van.* Below: *Detail from a mezzotint after George Morland's* The Benevolent Sportsman *showing how gypsies lived before they took to the road.*

picked out with panels of staring red, in which happily-constructed colours the concern shone brilliant. Neither was it a poor caravan drawn by a single donkey or emaciated horse, for a pair of horses in pretty good condition were released from the shafts and grazing on the grouzy grass. Neither was it a gipsy caravan, for at the open door (graced with a bright brass knocker) sat a Christian lady, stout and comfortable to look upon, who wore a large bonnet trembling with bows. And that it was not an unprovided or destitute caravan was clear from this lady's occupation, which was the very pleasant and refreshing one of taking tea . . . the steps being struck by George, and stowed under the carriage, away they went . . .

When they had travelled slowly forward for some short distance, Nell ventured to steal a look around the caravan and observe it more closely. One half of it—the moiety in which the comfortable proprietress was then seated—was carpeted, and so partitioned off at

Early 20th century photograph of a gypsy queen in the New Forest.

the further end as to accommodate a sleeping-place, constructed after the fashion of a berth on board ship, which was shaded, like the little windows, with fair white curtains, and looked comfortable enough, though by what kind of gymnastic exercise the lady of the caravan ever contrived to get into it, was an unfathomable mystery.

The other half served for a kitchen, and was fitted up with a stove whose small chimney passed through the roof. It held also a closet or larder, several chests, a great pitcher of water, and a few cooking utensils and articles of crockery.

The finest caravans were built by Gorgio craftsmen between about 1890 and 1914. Many types were constructed including the Reading, Ledge, Bow-top, Burton, Pot cart, Open-lot and Brush-van. Generally the Romany people preferred vans such as the Reading (the most famous makers of which were Dunton & Sons of Reading) that were slung between the wheels. This afforded less living accommodation but lowered the centre of gravity, providing greater stability in towing the van off the road into a wayside clearing. The showmen, on the other hand, favoured those vehicles with wheels under the body, such as the Burton (often but not exclusively made by Orton and Spooner of Burton-on-Trent). Dunton & Sons were the best known makers of caravans. Other makers among many who were 'Builders of Living Vans' included Williams of Leighton Buzzard, Bedfordshire; D. Macintosh of Upper Norwood, London; William Wheeler of Guildford, Surrey; C. H. King of Wisbech, Cambridgeshire; Leonard of Soham, Cambridgeshire; Fuller of St. Ives, Huntingdonshire; Skyes of Outwell, Norfolk; Godbolt of Norwich; Howcroft of West Hartlepool, County Durham; W. Watson and Herbert Varney, both of Belper, Derbyshire; Tong of Kearsley, Lancashire; Watts of Bridgewater, Somerset; H. Jones & Sons of Hereford, George Cox of Hereford; and the large Bristol Waggon and Carriage Works Ltd who, among their many activities, made Pullman railroad cars for America. The great Frederick Savage made caravans for the showmen who also bought roundabouts and other fairground machinery from his company. This is also true of much smaller firms like F. J. Thomas of Chertsey, Surrey, who in a trade card of 1908 advertised himself as a 'Builder of Living Vans, Round-abouts, Swing Boats, Dart and Ring Boards . . . All Kinds of Appliances for Travellers and Showmen . . . Hoop-la Maker and Patentee'.[1] Thomas also made knife-grinders' carts.

The 'gaily painted panels on which we looked with such innocent pride'[1] were the work of specialists. Dunton & Sons of Reading employed George Dunton (d. 1921) to

Left: *A model knifegrinder's cart in mahogany, inscribed VR and R. G. Lee, c1885.* Below left: *A bow-top gypsy caravan at the Appleby Fair, Westmorland in 1950.* Above: *An open-lot van at the same fair.* Below: *Gypsies on the road in an open-lot caravan c1920.*

do the painting and gilding. The Belper maker Herbert Varney had his workshops next door to the paintworks of A. Barnes & Sons, and these two firms often worked in partnership to make and decorate caravans, with Barnes himself doing the gilding which 'for the Gypsies it had to be Gold'.[5] In 1900 a caravan would cost between about £100 and £125, of which the painting would represent approximately one quarter. The wheels and chassis were traditionally painted yellow. The superstructure was painted in one predominent theme such as Indian red, with the chamfering and carving picked out in vermilion, blue and green. The Open-lot had little carving and the decoration was largely confined to elaborate painted designs and lining. Matt paints were used in this work which was finally given about two coats of varnish as a protection against the sun, wind and rain. In the late nineteenth century it was usual for the Gypsies to return to the makers who serviced the coachwork perhaps once every three years. Edward Harvey[2] makes it clear in his research before and after the 1914–18 War that many Romanies redecorated their vans themselves, and they also did some of the simpler repairs to the wood-work. For example, Thelmy Marshall is recorded as making a pair of side-screens. It was suggested to him that their design represented trees or foliage. Marshall responded 'No, just plain nothing, only sweet suent curves'.[2]

Wood-carving has always been a very special skill, and one that the Romany never mastered. It is no doubt for this reason that the Open-lot, the last caravan type to evolve, has no carved decoration beyond the plainest chamfering, which is simply a practical measure to reduce weight used to decorative effect. The caravan makers sub-contracted the wood-carving. Herbert Varney of Belper, worked in yellow pine of pattern-making quality—an unusual choice, as sycamore was more commonly used. Varney also used the work of Cyril Hookaby, who stopped in Belper each winter. Other carvers included Collier of Leeds, who worked for various North Country builders, and Gertnor, a German living in Hereford, who for thirty years carved decoration for caravans made by George Cox, and also had a reputation as an ecclesiastical wood-carver.

The van builders would assemble the caravans dry (without glue) and then send off the pieces that were intended for carving to the craftsmen. The purely decorative parts were normally carved from sycamore but elsewhere the wood demanded by the overall structure was used; wych-elm was used by Dunton for porch brackets, for example. Many of the carvers were of German and Italian origin, but the caravan never became so italianate in character as the early twentieth-century ice-cream cart. The ornament that these craftsmen carved included scrolls, curlicues, flowers (especially sunflowers for door panels), acanthus leaves, grapes and vines. Plant forms were usually painted 'proper'. Dunton is reputed to have added a bloom to carved bunches of grapes by the application of gold size and french chalk. The horse was inevitably a favourite motif as were horseshoes, whips and wheels. Tong of Kearsley built quite a number of waggons incorporating St George killing the dragon and the Prince of Wales feathers. Carving made these designs permanent even when the paint had been weathered away. In the early twentieth century the carving usually represented about fifteen per cent of the total cost of the van, which may be compared with an average of ten per cent for carved decoration on buildings at that time.

The Romany (full blood), the Poshrat (half blood), the Didikais (mixed blood, often applied loosely to mean non-Romany), the tinkers and brush sellers, the showmen and other itinerants, were all known to use caravans. The Romany was the last to adopt this type of home and the last to reject it.

The Fair

In medieval times fairs of both national and international significance were established as trading ventures, with amusement as a natural result but not as their *raison d'être*. These fairs were considered so important that merchants had the right of safe passage even between kingdoms that were at war. The organisers needed as large a potential public as possible. As a result, charters to hold fairs were granted for the feast days of saints, an association between the temporal nature of the fair with a spiritual celebration that probably goes back to Roman times. Cornelius Walford in his book *Fairs Past and Present* (1883)* states that he found 'Distinct traces of fairs of Roman origin at Helston, Cornwall, at Barnswell by Cambridge, at Newcastle-upon-Tyne and at several other places along the Roman Wall in Northumberland.' The granting of a Royal Charter to hold a fair bestowed on a community considerable status, and also generated wealth. Many fairs have slipped into abeyance but once there were a great many in the towns and larger villages of the British Isles. Some of these communities have prospered since and become large towns, others (such as Norton St Philip in Somerset) have declined leaving a great inn to serve as a reminder of former days of importance. Middleton Stoney in Oxfordshire, now a

*Walford was a lawyer, and this book deals not only with the history of fairs but also with their legal status.

BARTHOLOMEW FAIR, 1721.

Wild Beasts alive

Punch's Family

Fine Saucages

Top: *Bartholomew Fair in 1721.*
Above: *Three sections of a print dated September 17th 1800, showing various aspects of the fair.*

small village, is exceptional in that it received two charters to hold a fair. Undoubtedly the two greatest fairs in England were those of Sturbridge, near Cambridge, and St Bartholomew's at Smithfield, London.

Gradually entertainment and amusement gained in importance as trade conducted at fairs declined. The fair was given over to pleasure and, after 1851, the great govern-ment-sponsored international exhibitions became the centres of trade.

Eighteenth and even early nineteenth-century prints and paintings of fairs show them to have consisted of a series of simple booths, some with painted backcloths. With the rise of steam-power the roundabout or carousel assumed greater and greater importance, for the new means of pro-pulsion was capable of driving a great edifice burdened with wood-carving, mirror-glass and brass 'barley-suger'.

At the end of the fourteenth century at St Bartholomew's Fair, the Company of Parish Clerks[6] performed a miracle

play at Skinner's Well near Smithfield before Richard II and his court. Little is known of the 'props' used for these plays, which were very much a part of this great London fair. Dr W. L. Hildburg[7] argued that the small religious panels made of Nottingham alabaster provide some impression of the appearance of these plays, and this great collector pointed out how, in these sculptures, an element such as a nimbus is seen as a 'prop' firmly held by cherubs.

It is with the simple painted backcloth for a no less simple stall that the folk art of the fair may be seen to begin. In the absence of any known surviving examples I must refer yet again to Hogarth and in particular his Borough Fair at Southwark, which gives such a vivid impression of an eighteenth-century English fair:

> . . . (a fair, held, some time since, in the borough of Southwark, though now suppressed, on account of ill consequences attending such meetings, in very populous trading places.) Fairs were originally designed as general markets, though, now, through the licentiousness of the times, they are reduced to little else than seasons of dissipation, riot and intemperance . . .[6]

Hogarth has depicted a scene packed full of incident including:

> . . . upon the left . . . the fall of a scaffold, on which was assembled a strolling company, pointed out, by the paper lanthorn hanging in front to be that belonging to *Cibber* and *Bullock* . . . Here we see *merry-andrews*, monkeys, queens, and emperors, sinking in one general confusion . . . witness the boys and women gambling at the box and dice, the upright monkey, and, the little bag-piper dancing his wooden figures . . . Above this scaffold hangs a painting, the subject of which is the *stage-muting* . . . a scene-painter, having laid his brushes aside and taken up a cudgel . . . In the corner, is a man . . . hugging a bag of money, laughing at the folly of the rest . . . and behind, a monkey, perched upon a sign-iron supposed to be that of the *Rose-tavern* in *Drury-lane* . . . These paintings are, in general, designed to shew what is exhibited within . . . At the back of this plate is *Lee* and *Harper's* great booth, where by the picture of the wooden horse, we are told, is represented, the siege of Troy. The next paintings consist of the fall of Adam, and, Eve; and, in a scene in *Punch's* opera. Beneath, is a mountebank,

Above left: *A photograph of St Giles Fair in Oxford taken in 1905: this shows how elaborate fairground attractions had become in comparison with the simple diversions offered a century before.*

Left: *Engraving of Hogarth's* Southwark Fair, *dated 1733.*

Detail from Hogarth's Canvassing for Votes, *Plate 2 of* The Election, *published in 1757, showing 'Punch, Candidate for Guzzledown' throwing money to the crowds to buy votes.*

exalted on stage, eating fire, to attract the public attention; while his *merry-andrew*, behind, is distributing his medicine . . . let it suffice to say, it presents us many groups . . . [and] . . . shews us to what degeneracy the taste of the people is now arrived . . .[6]

In *The Election* Hogarth again illustrates a painted cloth such as is described above:

> In order to gain their [the electorate's] favour which is oftener effected by baubles and fights . . . he [the candidate] is supposed to entertain the village with a puppet show . . . The cloth bearing the *insignia* of this exhibition, is hoisted to the sign post, and is allusive to the subject we are upon; the lower part of which, represents, *Punch*, profusely, throwing money to the populace.[6]

Puppet and raree shows often appeared at fairgrounds. Joseph Strutt[8] suggested that puppets in England were developed from the 'autonomous motions' of religious figures such as the famous crucifix at Boxley, Kent, (described by Lambarde) or the mechanical figures used in a mechanism such as the knights on the clock inside Wells Cathedral. By the eighteenth century such automata seem to have been considered by European taste as suitable only for export. Edward Edwards describes James Bunk as one of those

> professional artists . . . who have contributed their feeble efforts toward supporting a spirit of enrichment and decoration among the inferior virtuosi. In that class of artists may be reckoned, the person here mentioned, who was a painter of no great powers. He was

chiefly employed by those who required subjects for mechanical movements, such as clocks for the East Indies, in which figures are represented, that are put in motion by the machine which they decorate.[9]

Mr Punch arrived in England from Italy in the seventeenth century and he is known to have made his appearance in London as early as 1666. *Punch's Moral Drama* was popularised by Robert Powell in the Italian version described by Addison in *The Spectator*.[10] Another eighteenth-century English puppet-master described some of his productions on his advertisements. The following example demonstrates the delight and splendid naïvety with which these shows were put together:

> At Crawley's Booth, over against the Crown Tavern in Smithfield, during the time of Bartholomew Fair, will be presented a little opera, called the Old Creation of the World, yet newly revived; with the addition of Noah's Flood; also served fountains playing water during the time of play . . . The last scene does present Noah and his family coming out of the Ark, with all the beasts two and two, and all the fowls of the air seen in prospect sitting upon trees, likewise over the ark is seen the Sun rising in a most glorious manner: moreover a multitude of Angels will be seen in double rank etc. etc.

Among other eighteenth-century puppet-masters (normally

Above: *A 19th century view of* A Punch & Judy Show outside The Stag's Head *by Thomas Smythe of Ipswich (1825–1926) (Detail only).* Below left: *Two carved and painted wooden marionettes from the middle of the 19th century.* Below and right: *Five Punch & Judy glove puppets, late 19th – early 20th centuries.*

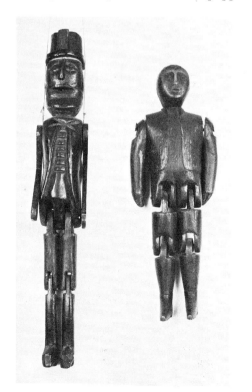

marionettes rather than glove puppets), are Martin Powell of Bath; Stretch of Dublin, who was followed at his death in 1744 by James Harvey; Charles Dibdin of Exeter, and Samuel Foot of London. Even Henry Fielding, using the pseudonym of Madame de la Nash, presented a satirical puppet-show in Panton Street in 1748.

Puppet-shows were at their most fashionable in the last quarter of the eighteenth century. Between 1770 and 1792 five distinct companies of Italian marionette performers presented seasons of Italian *fantoccini* in London. Shadow puppets appeared between 1775 and 1790 with performances of '*ombres chinoises*'.

Such sophisticated shows designed for the delectation of the fashionable were probably in marked contrast to the more boisterous and by this time thoroughly anglicised Mr Punch. Strutt, writing before 1801, records that 'In my memory, these shows consisted of a wretched display of wooden figures, barbarously formed and decorated without the least degree of taste or propriety'. However puppets were made that would have met with Strutt's approval. Charlotte Charke of St James, who opened her puppet-theatre in March 1738, hired a Mr Yeates to work from engraved portraits of prominent people of the day, carving marionettes of them for a total cost of £500. Yeates had once been a partner of Powell's son and a regular exhibitor of waxwork figures at London fairs. No doubt to eighteenth-

century sensibilities such as Strutt's these puppets were often 'barbarously formed and decorated' but there were clearly exceptions and, as George Speaight has pointed out, Strutt's 'severe comment has little validity for a generation that has discovered the charm of the English tradition in Popular Art'.[11] According to Smith,[12] 'the street exhibition of Punch and his wife delighted him [Nollekens] beyond expression . . . In this gratification, however our Sculptor did not stand alone, for I have frequently seen, when I have stood in the crowd, wise men laugh at the squeaking of Punch and have heard them speak of his cunning pranks with ecstacy'. Strutt[8] wrote that by his time puppets had 'become unpopular, and are frequented only by children.' Most surviving English glove puppets date from the nineteenth century and the best examples of Punch and Judy have heads, arms and feet of carved wood.

There is little doubt that the fairs of the past included many cruel 'entertainments' from which the surviving records and 'props' mercifully spare us. One of these, however, was the 'barbarous and wicked diversion of throwing at cocks [which] usually took place at the wakes and fairs held about Shrovetide, and especially at such of them as were kept on Shrove-Tuesday'. However, Strutt goes on to explain that when this 'amusement' was abolished 'the place of the living birds was supplied by toys made in the shape of cocks, with large and heavy stands of lead, at which the

boys on paying a trifling sum were permitted to throw as before . . .' These 'toys' were no doubt of carved wood, much like American decoy birds but as yet I have been unable to trace any examples with certainty.

It is remarkable paradox that the introduction of steam-power resulted in the ultimate decline of one folk art and the blossoming of another. As the steam-driven, iron-hulled ship became more and more common so the ship carvers became the wood sculptors of fiery steeds, of gorgeous dragons and of sprightly ganders for the fairground. And yet it was the power, the strength of steam that made it possible to drive the enormous edifices of 'people's baroque' that these rides and roundabouts had become. A late nineteenth-century Bristol carver is known to have made this transition. A. E. Anderson described himself on a brass plate as 'Ships Figurehead, Sign

Below left: Welsh or Chinese dragon from a scenic ride, c1880. The origin of these magnificently carved seats is obscure; the passenger sat facing backwards and was chased by the following dragon – up and down and round and round.

Below: A classical English galloper from a fairground ride c1910, probably made by Savages of Kings Lynn, Norfolk. The owner of the rider might paint the name of his wife, mother or daughter on these horses.

Above: *Late 19th century glove puppets: The Policeman, Judy and The Crocodile.*

Top left: *Remains of a peacock seat from a roundabout, c1900. Part of the figure is charred: it was rescued from being burnt with other out-of-date equipment at the end of the Second World War. This was the fate of many fine old fairground rides.*

Top right: *An unfinished galloper carved by A. E. Anderson of Bristol in the late 19th century.*

Above: *A. E. Anderson's sign was apparently adapted from a ship's name board. The label on the back states that he had workshops in Commercial Row, Mardyke (1865) and in Dock Gate Lane, Hotwells (1911).*

and Ornamental Carver'. A number of examples of Anderson's work survive in Bristol including the head of a roundabout horse. Preserved with them are a few wood-carving tools, but a craftsman of this quality would have needed at least 200 tools rather than the dozen or so that remain in the collection. What makes Anderson particularly interesting is that he regarded himself first and foremost as 'Anderson-Shipcarver' and it is thus and as nothing else that he describes himself on an enormous wooden sign. It seems that only circumstances drove him to do other work.

In an illustration of a small merry-go-round at a village fair, W. H. Pyne has left a record of the appearance of such 'whirligigs' before the widespread use of steam. The scale was inevitably small as its movement was provided by its passengers, much as the small roundabouts in child-

Above left: *a Merry-Go-Round in 1800.* Above: *Part of the centre of a large Marenghi 113-key organ; the figures are not the originals but indicate the range of carving and theme which fairground owners required to keep up with popular taste: the figure of the Boer War scout is a perfect example of the patriotism of the early 20th century.* Left: *Section of cresting from a late 19th century roundabout; the panel carries the number 16 on the back to simplify the assembly of the roundabout.* Below: *Two sections of a remarkable carved dropper board (c1880) which depicts not a race but a hunt in full cry. Dropper boards were hung around the centre of a ride to conceal the engine.*

ren's playgrounds to this day. Though it included some fine-looking legless horses 'drawing' a coach, it has clearly been designed to keep weight to a minimum, another reason why such devices were reserved for children. Howitt[3] confirms this observation as follows: 'Out of doors there are stalls of toys and sweetmeats, and whirligigs* for the

*These whirligigs are not to be confused with the American wind toys which have no equivalent in Britain.

children . . .' In the days before the steam-engine, the fair arrived by horse- power but steam, when it came, not only provided a means of transport, it was also the basis of a whole series of 'rides'. The crowning glory of these was the roundabout. In Britain the greatest maker of roundabouts was Frederick Savage and Co. Ltd. of Kings Lynn, Norfolk. This company of farm machinery manufacturers had developed a sideline into a profitable business. Frederick

Left: *Sides of chariots which used to form part of a scenic ride (c1910); they are only slightly carved but highly painted.*
Right: *St Giles Fair in Oxford at the end of the summer of 1895.*

Savage himself became a pillar of Victorian Kings Lynn and mayor of the town where his bronze figure still stands majestically in a frock-coat. So prosperous were Savages at one time that they opened a workshop in London at 26 Cross Street, Islington, employing Italian carvers. Templates for particular carvings were provided by the Kings Lynn headquarters, and on these, designs were drawn in London. An alternative design was usually placed on the reverse of the 'boasting'. The switchback made by Savages in 1922 for Leon Steppe was carved and gilded in a 'Louis XV' style. It was made with an engine salvaged from a switchback destroyed by fire in 1918. The new switchback took eleven months to complete and cost about £9,000. For this work twelve carvers from London and Birmingham worked with Arthur Bailey, Savage's regular carver. The related work of painting and gilding was sub-contracted. Charles Mumford of 'W. Sconce & Sons, Scenic Artists, Lynn' did the painting while the gilding was provided by R. & B. Frost (father and son), gilders who worked exclusively for Savages. In addition to the Savages other

makers are known, including Fenwick of Newcastle-upon-Tyne, William Keating of Wythenshaw and R. J. Woodfin of Tewkesbury. All these firms were concerned with maintenance and, in the case of a fire, reconstruction. The engines at present in W. H. & E. Ashley's roundabout built in the 1890s by Thomas Walker of Tewkesbury were not installed until 1946, but its hand-carved horses were supplied by Orton Sons and Spooner in 1925, although two of the original cockerels by Anderson of Bristol survive. Although many animals both real and fabulous made their appearance on the roundabout, the horse remained the most popular.

The continuing popularity of the roundabout or carousel as a 'ride' has carried this tradition into the twentieth century. The last quarter of the nineteenth century saw the roundabout and above all its carving and painted decoration at a high level of vitality, able to absorb contemporary events into a distinctly new visual vocabulary. The steam fair was both a product of industrialisation and a means of escape from it. In the late nineteenth century, miles and miles of soulless terraced housing were constructed, houses whose roofs of grey Welsh slate reflected in rain the sombre skies of industry and in summer glistened with coal grit. From and into this world moved the annual fair, more colourful than ever before, and without doubt more necessary.

The Circus

As with the roundabouts of the fairground, so with the circus. Both existed before the wide use of steam-power, but neither could flourish without it, for both needed something stronger than horse-power.

The logistics of transporting exotic and large wild animals in horse-drawn transport were considerable:

> Huge caravans incessantly arrive, with their wild beasts, theatricals, dwarfs, giants, and other prodigies and wonders. Then come trotting in those light, neat covered waggons, containing the contents of sundry bazaars that are speedily to spring up. As you go out of the town at any end, you meet caravan after caravan, cart after cart, long troops of horses tied head and tail, and groups of those wild and peculiar-looking people, that are as necessary to a fair as flowers are to May;— all kinds of strollers, beggars, gipsies, singers, players, dancers, players on harps, Indian jugglers, Punch and Judy exhibitors, and similar wandering artists and professors.[3]

The circus seems to have first made its appearance in England with the London establishment of Philip Astley (d. 1814). Astley was followed by Ducrow who was well known for feats of horsemanship, an aspect of the circus that was continued a generation later with Hengler's and Sanger's shows and which continues to the present day. The merging of this, the true circus, with other animals and clowns seems to have occurred in the second half of the nineteenth century. Howitt[3] is quite precise on this point:

> Wombwell's Menagerie displays all its gigantic animals on its scenes; Holloway's "Travelling Company of Comedians" are dancing with harlequin and clown in front of their locomotive theatre.

In other words the various elements of the circus were not originally combined in one 'locomotive' variety show under canvas. Dicken's *Dictionary of London 1879* lists 'Sanger's Amphitheatre' as being located at Westminster Bridge Road. Dickens describes the establishment as:

> A theatre and hippodrome . . . formerly known as Astley's, now in the hands of Messrs. Sanger, who have introduced a large menagerie element into the performances.

With steam the touring show became larger as also did the transport, which itself advertised the arrival of the circus. The greatest exponent of circus publicity was undoubtedly the American P. T. Barnum. In England on a smaller scale, circus waggons were decorated with voluptuous carving and shaded lettering, an art form and advertising medium born of the steam-engine and improved road systems.

Below: Rowlandson and Pugin's view of Astley's circus, c1810. Bottom: Day's Menagerie with 'Bears, Wolves and Hyenas' as it appeared at St Giles Fair in Oxford in 1895.

The Canals

The art of the narrow boat, like that of the fair and circus, was a product of the second half of the nineteenth century and, like the caravans, canal boats were originally horse-drawn. They all established powerful traditions within a generation: a remarkable achievement.

The first post-Roman canal built in Britain was the Bridgewater Canal opened in 1761. Little is known of the origin of the men who dug the canals or of the navigators who surveyed their route. The word 'navigator' was, according to the *Shorter Oxford Dictionary*, shortened around 1832 to 'navvy' and its meaning corrupted to describe the labourer who dug the canals rather than the man who surveyed them. Some of these labourers were no doubt men who had left the land because of the Enclosure Acts; others were perhaps gypsies; others, Irish immigrants. These men, like the colliers with their brutalising lives, were feared by the communities through which they passed, drinking and womanising to excess. It was perhaps from them, as well as from those with existing skills in navigating rivers and coastal waters, that the canal people were drawn. It has

A bargee decorating a watercan.

even been suggested that Dutch canal folk brought with them their particular culture. Whatever their origin, it is certainly true that their artistic tradition did not appear until the canals began to decline in the 1830s. Only when whole families 'manned' these boats did the desire for a water-borne home produce the castles and rose painting now inseparably associated with narrow boats.

In the heyday of the canals, between 1761 and 1834, the narrow boats were strictly utilitarian. A boat would be operated by a man and a boy who lived at home or in hostels ashore. A by-law of the Stourbridge Canal of 1789 insisted that a boat passing through a lock should be manned by two men and a boy. In those days of flourishing commerce on the canals the boats were owned for the most part by large companies, such as Pickfords. This firm had begun life in the haulage business with a fleet of road waggons, but by the 1790s they were important canal-boat owners who in addition leased warehouses and wharves. This company and others were proud of their efficiency, which is celebrated on a blue painted earthenware plate, made between 1800 and 1820, which bears the following verse:

Pickford, Beach and Snell's are jolly Lads, and true ones:
Kenworthy, and Worthington's, you'll likewise find true blue ones:
Wakeman, Green and Ames, amiss you'll never find Sirs,
Holt's Crocket and Salkeld's, will sail fast as the wind Sirs,
True Harted and Jolly ones you'll find with Heath and Crawley,
Sturland's Henshall's, Alkin's too can likewise use their mauley
So likewise can the Boatmen all, and drink their can of flip Sirs
They'll drink their grog, and toast their lass, and then they'll crack the whip Sirs.[13]

In addition to the large companies' fleets of boats, there were a few 'Number Ones' owned by individuals. In the early 1840s, when Pickfords transferred their business to the railways, the number of one-man businesses increased. The 1841 census revealed a total of 28,166 people in the canal business, and of these the barge people represented 23,226 men and 132 women in England and Wales. With the decline of the canals a boat could support only one wage-earning person; it was the unpaid wives and children that made possible the continued use of Britain's canals and it was these families that begat the tradition for stern cabins brightly painted with roses and castles. The coloured engravings made by Thomas Shepheard in 1827 and 1828 of

Typical Midland narrow boat with decorated woodwork and watercans.

Above: *Stool from a narrow boat's cabin.*

Above right: *Two canal boat dippers, used to fetch water from the canal; the less accomplished treatment of flowers on the right-hand example suggests that it is the earlier of the two.*

Right: *In the Lion's Den by W. H. Rogers (11in x 14in). The mother of the cub is, of course, a tiger. If the lion is indeed the father the cubs would be 'ligers'. Lions and tigers mate only in captivity.*

the Regent's Canal show that at that time narrow boats were simply decorated with diamonds and other symbols presumably taken from playing-cards: emblems which survived in the later and literal flowering of this folk art. John Hollingshead in his *Household Words* (1858) was the first to describe this decoration in print.

The origin of the playing-card motifs is clear. The roses and castles are more of a mystery. They appear to derive from the folk art of eastern Europe, and were perhaps introduced by the Romanies. Certainly the 'onion-domed' churches and dramatic landscapes are foreign to England, likewise the roses that are neither of York nor of Lancaster, nor even derived from nature. In canal boatyards dotted about the country the painting was carried on, for example, by the Nurser Brothers of Braunston, Walker's of Rickmansworth, Faulkner's of Leighton Buzzard and Yarwood's of Northwich. They and their work were well known to the boat people and they enjoyed considerable status. In painting, each panel was treated with two priming coats, two undercoats, two top coats of green, black, red or blue and one coat of varnish. Only then could those splendid calligraphic roses be applied, roses that were not so much painted as performed, with the skill of some dextrous game. Each blossom was composed on a coloured disc with a series of unerring 'dashes' of colour, each 'dash' representing a petal and each petal separate from its neighbours. As with most folk art the clients wanted bright colours, and they got them. Not for them the decadent desire for the patination of age: as soon as that set in it was time to have everything repainted — cabin, water-cans, dippers, nose-bowl,

seatboard, navigation-lamp, coal-box and cabin-block. Associated with all of these were the tillers decorated with ropework, horse harnesses and brasses, and the Measham-ware teapots, brown and rather dowdy but relieved by white ribbons in the ceramic, bearing names and mottoes.

1   L. G. Sanger, *Seventy Years a Showman*, 1926.
2   *Journal of the Gypsy Lore Society*, vol. 17, no. 3, 'English Gypsy Caravan Decoration' by Edward Harvey.
3   William Howitt, *Rural Life of England*, 1840.
4   *The English Gypsy Caravan*, illus. page 101.
5   *The English Gypsy Caravan*, page 109.
6   *Hogarth Moralized*, London, 1767.
7   *Archaeologia*, vol. 93, pp 51–102, 'English alabaster carvings as records of the medieval religious drama' by W. L. Hildburg.
8   Joseph Strutt, *Sports and Pastimes of the People of England*, 1801.
9   Edward Edwards, *Anecdotes of Painters*, London, 1808, page 32.
10 *The Spectator*, vol. I, no. XIV, 1711.
11 *Punch and Judy—a History*, Studio Vista, London, 1955, 1970.
12 J. T. Smith, *Nollekens and his Times*, 1919 ed.
13 Illustrated in *Country Life*, 22 December 1955, in 'History in Ceramics' by Stanley W. Fisher.

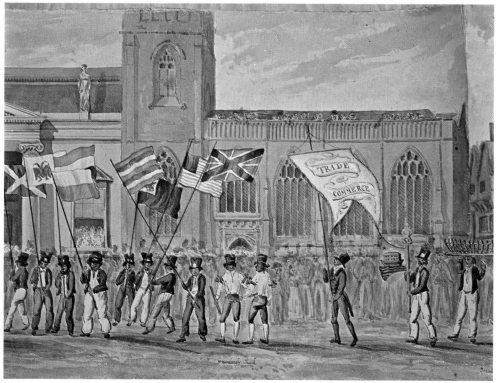

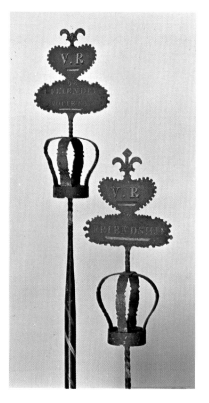

Processions and Pageants

According to Burton in his *Anatomy of Melancholy* (1660), processions and pageants were not only popular, they were also an effective safety-valve:

> They [the Londoners] take pleasure to see some pageant or sight go by, as at a coronation, wedding, and such solemn niceties, to see an ambassador or a prince received and entertained with masks, shows, and fireworks. The country hath also his recreations, as May-games, feasts, fairs, and wakes . . . Let them [the common people] freely feast, sing, dance, have puppet-plays, hobby-horses, tabers, crowds [ancient violin], and bagpipes . . . Plays, masks, jesters, gladiators, tumblers, and jugglers, are to be winked at, lest the people should do worse than attend them.[1]

Whatever psychological needs such pageants met, it is certain that many took place. In the early sixteenth century, the part of the City of London known as Leadenhall was devoted to the painting, construction and storage of the 'props' and effects of the City's pageants.

Pageants could also be static. At certain points in the City, tableaux would be set up—temporary buildings representing castles, palaces, gardens, rocks or forests inhabited as occasion demanded by nymphs, fauns, satyrs, gods, goddesses, angels, devils, savages, saints, knights, buffoons,

Opposite, top left: A hand-painted watercan of galvanised iron; earlier examples were usually painted on tin-plated iron.

Top right: A Measham ware teapot. Much of this 'barge ware' was made near Church Gresley and at the Victoria Pottery near Woodville, Derbyshire; it is called Measham ware because it was sold at a shop on the Ashby-de-la-Zouche canal at Measham.

Bottom left: Detail from a watercolour panorama on a paper roll by Henry Smith, The Chairing of Mr Bright *(1820) showing an axe similar to that illustrated opposite page 40. The panorama measures 6in by 160in.*

Bottom right: A pair of Friendly Society staves made for the village of Kingston Deverell in Wiltshire in the early 19th century; painted iron and wood, overall height 8ft.

dwarfs, dragons and giants. The giants were particularly popular. They were found throughout north-west Europe: in Belgium at Antwerp, Ath, Brussels, Dinant, Grammont, Hasselt, Malines, Namur, Nivells, Ostend and Ypres; in France at Lille and Douai; in Holland and the Black Forest. In England the most famous giants were undoubtedly Gog and Magog, characters associated with the legendary foundation of London by Brutus, the great-grandson of Aeneas, who on landing at Totnes, Devon, overcame a race of evil giants. In *The Gigantic History of Two Famous Giants in Guildhall, London,*[2] published in 1741, the following information appears:[3]

> Before the present giants [of carved wood] inhabited Guildhall, there were two giants made only of wicker-work and pasteboard, put together with great art and ingenuity: and those two terrible giants had the honour yearly to grace my Lord Mayor's Show, being carried in great triumph at the time of the pageants; and when that eminent annual service was over, remounted their old stations in Guildhall—till by reason of their very great age, old Time, with the help of a number of city rats and mice, had eaten up all their entrails. The dissolution of the two old, weak and feeble giants, gave birth to the two present substantial and majestic giants, who by order, and at the city charge, were formed and fashioned. Captain Richard Saunders, an eminent carver in King Street, Cheapside, was their father, who, after he had completely finished, clothed and armed these his two sons, they were immediately advanced to those lofty stations in Guildhall, which they have peaceably enjoyed over since 1708*

John Smith in *Nollekens*, when speaking of the importance of scale as opposed to mere size, writes:

> I well recollect my play-fellow, John Deare [1759–98], the Sculptor, powerfully maintaining that grandeur never depended upon magnitude. A preposterously large figure like Gog or Magog in Guildhall, or the giant and giantess of Antwerp, would without dignity,

*They were destroyed by bombing on 29 December 1940 and the present figures are replacements.

The INDUSTRIOUS 'PRENTICE Lord-Mayor of London.

Proverbs CHAP: III. Ver: 16.
Length of days is in her right hand, and in her left hand Riches and Honour.

Plate 12.

The Lord Mayor's Procession as depicted by Hogarth in Plate 12 of The Industrious Prentice, *published in 1747.*

breadth of style and just proportion, exhibit nothing beyond a mass of overwhelming lumber . . .

Richard Saunders (d. 1735) who carved the firwood figures of Gog and Magog was in his day a very well known sculptor in wood and Captain of the City Trained Bands. He had been apprenticed to Jonathan Maine (1680–1709) in 1675 and became free in 1682. He worked for the Earls of Ashburnham and did a great deal of work for the City of London, including the 'carving about the City eighteen-oared barge'.[4]

It was the predecessors of Saunders' figures that were more in the nature of folk art. The Salisbury giant is the only member of this species to survive and is apparently the original that first made its appearance in 1496 at the time of Henry VII's visit to Clarendon. The face, which is carved in walnut, has been reworked a number of times. The figure represents St Christopher and was originally

owned and carried in processions by the Merchant Taylors' Guild. The giant has been re-dressed on numerous occasions including, in 1784, in celebration of peace after the American War of Independence. 'The Giant was entirely new dressed, his coat alone taking 34 yards of cloth.' With his huge wooden dagger (eighteenth century?) and sword carried by a sword-bearer or 'whiffler', he customarily made his appearance on the streets of Salisbury in midsummer, together with Hob Nob the dragon clearing the way. Norwich has a similar dragon known as 'Old Snap' who was active from 1451 to 1835. These dragons may well be related to the hobby horses of such places as Padstow, Cornwall, the Hoddening Horse of Cheshire and Kent, or the Mari Lwyd (Grey Mary) that visited houses in Wales

Above and above right: *19th century watercolours of the wooden effigies of Gog and Magog carved by Richard Saunders in 1708.* Right: *A Mari Lwyd procession in Llangynwyd, Glamorgan, c1910.*

at Christmas, and maybe even the pantomime horse. If so, these figures go back to the ancient ethnology of Britain. At various times, as religious and moral standards shifted, attempts were made to suppress these mysterious figures from our tribal past. Once Chester had four and Coventry two processional giants.

In 1564 Chester's pageant consisted of 'four giants, one unicorn, one dromedary, one luce [pike], one camel, one ass, one dragon, six hobby-horses, and sixteen naked boys.'[5] This pageant was discontinued during the Commonwealth and all these gorgeous figures destroyed. With the Restoration,

67

All things were made new, by reason of the ould modells were broken . . . For finding all the materials, with the workmanship of the four great giants, all to be made new, as neere as may be lyke as they were before [a tribute to the strength of tradition], at five pounds a giant the least that can be, and four men to carry them at two shillings and six pence.[6]

These giants were made of metal hoops, deal boards, nails, pasteboard, paper, buckram and sized cloth, all of which was coloured and gilded with, in addition, 'arsnick to put into the paste to save the giants being eaten by rats.' George Puttenham in *The Art of English Poesie* (1589) describes

these midsommer pageants in London, where, to make the people wonder, are set forth great and uglie Gyants marching as if they were alive and armed at all points, but within they are stuffed full of browne paper and tow, which the shrewd boys under-peering, do guile-fully discouer and turn to great derision.

After the decline of the craft guilds as arbiters and representatives of their respective crafts, and before the full-blooded emergence of the trades unions, clubs or friendly societies were of some importance in rural communities. Both men and women had their societies, which also served as banks for the common people. These societies held at least one general meeting each year, usually on Whit Monday, and the members processed to the village church for a special service. Howitt, in his *Rural Life of England* (1840) describes one of these occasions when the friendly society staves were much in evidence.

I see the clubs, as they are called, coming down the village; a procession of its rustic population all in their best attire. In front of them comes bearing the great banner,* emblazoned with some fitting scene and motto, old Harry Loman the blacksmith, deputed to that office for the brawny strength of his arms, and yet, if the wind be stirring, evidently staggering under its weight, and finding enough to hold it aloft. There it floats its length of blue and yellow, and on its top nods the huge posy of peonies, laburnum flowers and lilacs, which our own garden has duly furnished. Then comes sounding the band of drums, bassoons, hautboys, flutes, and clarionets: then the honorary members—the freeholders of the place—the sage apothecary and the priest . . . Now the banner and the gilded tops of their wands are seen glancing between the hedge-row trees . . .

Even in Howitt's day these occasions were beginning to decline, for he writes:

*An early reference to the precursor of the trade union banner.

Early 19th century shipwright's processional device in painted wood representing a caulking mallet and caulking irons. One example of a series of large scale shipwright's tools used in processions in the City of Bristol. Caulking is the process of sealing the joints between a ship's planks by forcing in oakum and tar. A caulker's mallet is traditionally made from lignum vitae and split to prevent it from 'ringing' in use.

. . . the utilitarian spirit, especially during periods of general distress, has induced many of them to give up their bands, banners, and ribbons, and to throw the money thus saved into the general stock.

Most of these West Country poleheads were made of brass in centres such as Bristol. Some were made of glass by the Nailsea glassworkers, but most important were the larger and more elaborate examples made in tin. These were gilded and painted and sometimes bore the name of the village.

1 Quoted by Joseph Strutt, *Sports and Pastimes of the People of England*, 1801, page 19.
2 *The Gigantic History* is a chapbook, measuring 2½ ins. x 1½ ins.
3 Quoted by William Hone in *Ancient Mysteries Described*, London, 1823.
4 Rupert Gunnis, *Dictionary of British Sculptors 1660–1851*, London, 1951.
5 *Harleian Mss*, 2125.
6 Quoted by Strutt (see 1 above), page 31.

Ships
and the Mariner

The ship has from antiquity been a means of trading and an instrument of war and was in both capacities an outward and visible sign of a nation's wealth and strength. Such national pride found artistic expression through the wood-carver and painter. Only the humble fishing-smack, which seldom entered foreign ports, was left comparatively un-adorned. Ancient though this art form was, it gave way by degrees to the emergence in the mid-nineteenth century to the iron-hulled ship driven by steam.

The seafarer was not simply the client of the craftsman's art; he too was creative. Apart from the skills of rope-

Below left and centre: Two sperm whale teeth forming a pair engraved with allegorical figures of Hope and Britannia. Right: A carved pine figurehead probably from a small British warship or merchantman, c1845.

knotting and macramé that grew out of his trade, he painted and embroidered pictures of the ship or ships on which he served. The whalers of America and Britain engraved whales' teeth and bone and used this material to make on board ship numerous household articles known as 'scrim-shaw', but only British seamen seem to have produced woolwork pictures.

The homecoming sailor brought mysterious objects from fabled lands, and sometimes also his own paintings of the people and places that he had seen. Many of the engravings that appear in early volumes describing voyages of discovery were derived not only from drawings by professional artists, who it is known accompanied such expeditions, but also from the work of amateurs. Captain James Cook himself produced primitive drawings that were processed by the engraver into a form acceptable to eighteenth-century taste.

Ropework was an extension of the seaman's skills and with it he made 'Turk's head knots' and 'ocean mats'. Even the sail canvas was worked into samplers of drawn-thread work.

Idleness and illiteracy were considered by Victorians to be great social evils. The Victorian sailor in his shipboard moments of idleness demonstrated the virtues of leisure as used by those who were often illiterate.

Ship Decoration

The figureheads of splendid naïvety, the Venus forms full-bosomed and pink-nippled, are strangely enough a largely Victorian expression of unsuppressed *joie-de-vivre* in an art form whose days were numbered.

The stern-castle and the forecastle of medieval ships limited decoration to painted work. Even when these fore and aft structures disappeared, painted decoration remained for a while almost the sole embellishment. Surviving drawings of Tudor vessels, such as those in the *Ancient English Shipwrightry* (Pepys Mss. Collection), do however show what appear to be carved figureheads (see illustrations of what is presumed to be the *Ark Royal* of 1587).

By the early seventeenth century, ship carving was becoming prominent if not dominent, as can be seen by consulting that amazing survival of the period, the Swedish ship *Vasa*. This vessel was designed by a Dutchman, Maarten Redtmer, and as the Dutch were a great influence on British shipbuilding practice at this time, she is of particular significance to us, the more so as the evidence for this period is so meagre. Contemporary pictures and models of British ships may permit one to conclude that a vessel like the *Sovereign of the Seas*, launched in 1637, though princely in her carving and gilding, was deficient as a piece of naval architecture. The decoration was probably designed by Van Dyck. Such ships were made for show, or, as Sir William Monson expressed it (1618), for 'honour':

> The former Navies had but four Royal Ships which were held sufficient for the honour of the State.[1]

As the state *was* the monarch, the Royal Arms formed a dominant motif on Royal Naval ships throughout the seventeenth and most of the eighteenth centuries. For two centuries the lion was almost the only subject for figureheads. In contrast to Tudor practice, colour was used sparingly, though gilding was excessively applied. Because the monarch was directly concerned with his navy, the

Print showing the dimensions of the Sovereign of the Seas, *built in 1637 and renamed the* Royal Soveraign.

style of all decoration was in the dominant idiom of the court.

The prevailing standards of the court were also applied to river craft such as the state barges, whether they were constructed for princes or livery companies.[2] By the standards of the day these vessels were expensive not only to build but also to maintain. One of the most remarkable state barges ever constructed was designed for Frederick, Prince of Wales, in 1732 by William Kent. It was built by John Hall, with carving by John Richards* and painting and gilding by Paul Pettit, at a total cost of £1,000 8s. 7d. It was so extravagant that Prince Frederick was persuaded to use it only because it was 'good natured to entertain the people'. The people of London were often entertained by water-borne pageants—the Lord Mayor's, for example—with the livery company barges much in evidence. Such pageants are known to have taken place as early as 1454, but were discontinued in 1857. The City of London must have regarded these occasions as being of some consequence,

*On Grinling Gibbons' death in 1722 John Richards (1671-1759) was appointed by George I to 'The Place and Office of Our Master Sculptor and Master Carver in Wood [at] Eighteen Pence per day.'

70

for it employed in 1711 no less a sculptor than Richard Saunders (who had carved Gog and Magog for the Guildhall) for 'carving about the City eighteen-oared barge' for a fee of £25.

In 1703 and again in 1796 the Admiralty determined that extravagant bow and stern decoration should go. That it was necessary to announce this ruling twice shows the power of the seaman's traditions and his superstition. The decision of 1703 was disregarded, as reference to contemporary ship models makes clear. A model of the Royal George (1756) in the National Museum, Greenwich, has a stern as flamboyant as a late Victorian pub or theatre. Even as late as 1799 *A New Book of Ornaments . . . in . . . Carving . . . Ships* was published in London. William Sutherland in his *The Ship Builders Assistant* (London 1711) includes a chapter entitled 'Of Beauty' which, while it certainly deals with the overall form of the ship, is no less concerned with surface decoration. The first sentence of this chapter reads, 'This Branch teaches to deck or adorn a Ship or Such like Machine, with that Symmetry of the

Parts as to render it agreeable to every Spectator', and then, after referring to decoration and with a side-swipe at the excesses of the previous century. Sutherland adds 'but with this Proviso, that the Beautifying may be no Detriment to the other good Properties'. He was an experienced shipwright:

> 'Tis the product of 32 Years Study and Experience for 'tis very well known that I have been so long imploy'd in her Majesty's Service and that of her Royal Predecessors; so that I may say I was in a manner born a Seaman, as most of my ancestors were. My Grandfather was Foreman to the Shipwrights in her Majesty's Yard at Deptford* 30 Years, my Uncle Mr Bagwell died Master Builder of her Majesty's Yard at Portsmouth, my Father and several of my Relations were Master Carpenters in the Royal Navey.

High standards of craftsmanship were attained not just by long apprenticeships but also by the general surroundings in which such men as Sutherland were reared. High quality materials were also important. In 1764 Thomas Searle of

The Lord Mayor's Procession by water in 1683, from a painting by John Griffier.

*It is tempting to wonder if Sutherland or his grandfather knew Grinling Gibbons who was discovered by John Evelyn at Deptford.

Lambeth and Nathaniel Clarkson, painter and gilder, made a new state barge for the Merchant Taylors. It was constructed of 'White English oak free from Redness, Rot, Sap and Prejudicial Knots' with floorboards of 'Christiana deal' (Baltic pine). Sutherland describes—

> how to beautify her [a ship] with Rules for Shaping the Head and Stern or Galleries . . . . All of which will be very necessary to be known and agreed upon, to save the trouble of Alternatives and garnishing Ships divers times, which is very chargeable.

To help the shipbuilder in this respect he illustrates designs for both a lion figurehead and stern decoration, and provides 'boasting' drawings to assist in assembling the necessary scantlings. The book contains a fascinating 'Explanation of the Principal Terms used in this Treatise', many of which concern ship carving:

> *Brackets*; generally carved Figures for Ornaments.
> *Chok*; a small Piece of Timber fitted to a larger to make out the substance required.
> *Dead-eyes*; Pieces having three Holes through, in which the Lanyards of the Shrouds are reeved.
> *Deep Land-mark*; the Horizontal Parallel of the Surface of the Water, when the Ship has every thing aboard that she is to carry.*
> *Draught*; the Model or Figure of a Ship, or any of her Parts described upon Paper.

*The Plimsoll Line was introduced in 1876. Samuel Plimsoll was born in the port of Bristol in 1824 and died in 1898.

> *Druxy*; Plank or Timber decayed and Spungy.
> *To Dub*; work with an Addice.
> *To Eek*; to fit a Part for the fashioning out another more material, as in the Supporter of the Cat-head and the Cheeks of the Head, where the Eeking is only applied to continue the Shape and Fashion of the Part, and for little other Service.
> *Knee*; a crooked Piece of Timber that has one Branch out off the Bending, and the other remaining makes the Bend or Knee Timber.
> *Nog*; a Trenel drove in at the foot of each Shore, or the Props that support the Ship in the Nature of trigging the Shores.*
> *Overlaunching*; Splicing or Scarfing one Piece of Timber to another, to make firm work.
> *Quick-work*; that part of a Ship's Sides within and without Board, above the Channel-wales and Decks.

*'Brick nogging' on the other hand is the non-structural brickwork found in timber frame houses and being non-structural is used decoratively.

Below left: *A plate from* The Ship Builder's Assistant *(1711) by William Sutherland, Section III: 'Essay on Marine Architecture Beauty or the Outward Ornament, & Garnishing of the parts in view'.*
Below right: *Detail from Hogarth's* Canvassing for Votes, *Plate 2 in the series* The Election *(1757) showing a lion figurehead.*

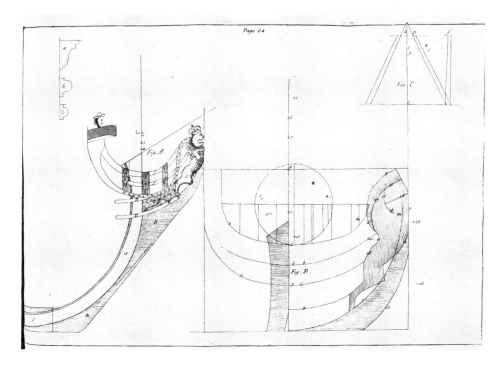

'Tis commonly perform'd with Fir-Deal, which don't require the fastening nor the Time to work it, as the other parts, but is Quicker done.

To Reconcile; to make one Piece of Work answer to the Uniformity of the other next to it, and more particularly in reverting Curves.

Scantling; the Length, Breadth, Depth or Thickness of any part of the ship.

Shaken Plank or Timber; such as is full of Clefts, and will neither bear calking nor fastening.

To Strike; to draw a Line, or delineate a Circle.

Tasting a Plank or Timber; Chipping of it with an Addice to try the Defects.

Thick-stuff; all Plank (as it may be termed) which is thicker than 4 Inches.*

The work of the ship carver has long been respected. There are instances of decoration being removed from an unseaworthy vessel to be attached to its successor. The 1718 state barge of the Merchant Taylors re-used the carving from its predecessor of 1668. At other times ship carvings, particularly figureheads, found themselves no longer terminating the elegant curves of a 'ship of the line' but instead gracing and advertising some landlocked inn by way of a sign. In Hogarth's second plate in his series of three entitled *The Election* a woman is shown counting money while 'she sits upon the head of an old ship, fixed at the door, as is commonly seen at public houses, which represents a lion ready to devour a flower-de-luce, (the French arms); emblematical of the natural animosity that, constantly, subsists between the two nations, *England and France.*'[3] At Martlesham, Suffolk, the Red Lion uses just such a figurehead as its sign to this day.

Although craftsmen's methods changed very little, a high level of sophistication characterised the work of seventeenth- and eighteenth-century ship carvers. A 'genteel, workmanlike and reasonable manner'[4] was typical. There were however exceptions. Under *Naval Architecture* in *The Complete Dictionary of Arts and Sciences* (edited by the Rev. Temple Henry Croker and others, London 1764) may be found these remarks:

> There is no certain rule for laying them [ships] down; this is left entirely to the fancy and taste of the artist, which, as we have more than once observed, is not often of the most delicate degree, or corrected by truth and judgement; witness the barbarous and unnatural mixture of Gothic and Chinese ornaments "clumsey heroes and fat headed gods" on the same ship, the monstrous issue of a savage conception and way ward

*Standards change; today, any plank in excess of 3 in would be termed 'thick stuff'.

The Red Lion, Martlesham, Suffolk could almost be the same lion as the one drawn by Hogarth.

> genius, as deformed and perverse as their own cant timbers.*

Towards the end of the eighteenth century the quantity of decoration borne by ships was reduced, and improved knowledge of naval architecture resulted in the production of vessels that had more beautiful overall lines where the

*'The cant or diagonal ribband so called because it cuts the body plane in a diagonal'—from *A Treatise on Ship Building* by Mungo Murray. London 1765.

carving was used to punctuate rather than obliterate the ship. Corresponding with this development was the decline in the use of a lion as an inevitable figurehead for a ship of the line. Instead such ships began to carry carving that bore some affinity to their names. Though few figureheads survive from before 1800, the Maritime Museum at Buckler's Hard, Hampshire, contains a number of drawings of the period by Henry Adams, the Master Ship Builder at Buckler's Hard from 1749 to 1790, who had been apprenticed at Deptford. One drawing is a design for the figurehead of *HMS Gladiator*, a helmeted warrior holding a sword, and another is of *HMS Heroine*, a romantic female figure holding a dagger.

The overall character of figureheads was conditioned by the design of the whole ship. First the beak-head, and then through the eighteenth century the bow, became more and more vertical. Finally, with the introduction of the clipper ship in the nineteenth century, the bow became horizontal again. Such changes were easily assimilated by carvers working in the shipyards, but the introduction of the iron hull was more of a problem. Most important of these was Brunel's *Great Britain*, which went on her maiden voyage in 1845. She nevertheless had her full complement of carving at stern and head, linked by a band of carved rope. Such decoration continued in use until comparatively recently,

Above: *Drawings by Henry Adams of figureheads for HMS* Gladiator *(50 guns) and HMS* Heroine *(32 guns).* Right, top: *An early example of a ship's figurehead.* Centre: *Nelson, a figurehead in carved and painted wood.* Right: *Figurehead from Foster's Boatyard, Cambridge, known to be the work of a deaf and dumb carver from London. This yard operated from 1865 to 1910.* Bottom, left: *A figurehead dated 1861.* Centre: *A figurehead which like many others has survived through the West Country practice of erecting them in memory of lost ships and their crews;* Right: *Figurehead of the ironclad HMS* Warrior, *built in 1861.*

especially in out of the way parts of the world. In the opening sentences of *Lord Jim*, Conrad describes a ship chandler's in the Far East 'where you can get everything to make her [a ship] seaworthy and beautiful, from a set of chain-hooks for her cable to a book of gold-leaf for the carvings of her stern'. This quotation makes it clear that running repairs were carried out on ship decoration in the course of a voyage.

Eventually and inevitably, ships of metal powered by steam abandoned both carving and sails, and no longer were the great ocean-going vessels made by men like Sutherland with their 'Variety of both Matter and Art'.[5]

Seamen's Crafts

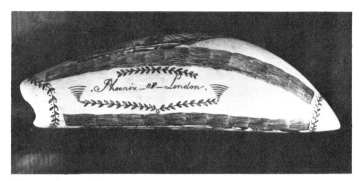

Two views of a sperm whale tooth showing the whaler Phoenix *of London with a carcase alongside. The process of flensing is in progress and a large 'blanket' of blubber is being stripped off the whale and taken on board with a tackle.*

Although Sutherland described himself on the title-page of his book as 'Shipwright and Mariner', this combination was unusual. The men who went down to the sea in ships were not generally the same as those who built them. The ship's carpenter and blacksmith were possible exceptions, and it was they who were much involved with the seamen's crafts produced on board during times of leisure, using any reasources available—from a coconut in the tropics to a whale's tooth in the Arctic. Reading was not then a common accomplishment. Due to the nature of the sailor's life, his art was international in character, and it is often difficult to be sure of the source of the various objects. This position is complicated by the fact that things made in all parts of the world were taken or sent almost anywhere else.

In post-Roman northern Europe, when elephant ivory was more difficult to obtain, English and Scandinavian craftsmen worked in walrus or morse ivory. The mystical and medical properties of the narwhal tusk, thought to be from the unicorn, were also important in medieval Europe, and both plain and elaborately carved examples survive from those times.

From the time of the great voyages of discovery, the nautilus shell and the coconut have been brought back to Europe by seamen. Engraved and silver mounted, the finest of these trophies were used to grace a nobleman's table as a 'salt' or 'nef'. Such objects as these, then, were transformed by men working on shore. J. T. Smith, in *Nollekens and his Times* describes a lesser such craftsman who had the temerity to approach Mrs Nollekens with a view to making 'professional application to her husband':

> . . . a person who cut castles, rocks, and mountains upon the backs of shells, and all with a common pen knife . . . You might as well praise the carvings upon a Wycherley comb*, so carefully preserved by the collector of old china and such gimcracks . . .[6]

Scrimshaw. The origin of scrimshaw—the whalers' craft of making objects of the ivory obtained from the whales they caught—is as uncertain as that of the word itself.

*Wycherley wig-combs were named after the Restoration playwright. They were made in Jamaica of engraved tortoiseshell and were fashionable in the last quarter of the seventeenth century (see article by Geoffrey Wills on 'Jamaican engraved tortoiseshell wig-combs' in *The Connoisseur Year Book,* 1957). The character, though not the period or the subject matter (which is distinctly tropical, with palms, etc.) of this engraving is similar to engraved baleen.

Some say that 'skrimshander', 'scrimshouter', 'scrimshorn' or 'scrimshaw' originates from a Dutch word meaning 'one who lazes around'. This is a fairly convincing argument, as it was in their moments of leisure that British, American and other sailors produced this work, but it is not known where the tradition began. Edward Stackpole and others have implied that scrimshaw is an American art form, but this seems unlikely.

The whale teeth were smoothed with sharkskin and engraved with a sailor's needle (an awl-like instrument). The engravings were of anything from ships to 'pin-ups', the designs often based on a printed source and pricked through on to the ivory. The engraving was then blackened with Indian ink, lamp-black or tar. At times, coloured inks were used for emphasis. Red was the most popular colour, but blue, green and orange were also used. Once the engraving was complete and the lines filled, the whole tooth was finished by polishing with ash, pumice-powder or whitening.

This purely decorative work was only one type of scrim-

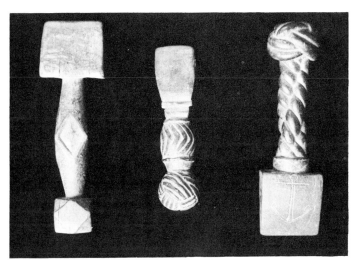

Left: *Decorated stay busks, one made from whale ivory, the other, marked 'P.F.' from baleen, the horny plates found in the mouth of the baleen whale.* Top: *A tail stamp carved from baleen and used to record each whale killed.* Above: *Sailmaker's seam rubbers made for use on board ship.*

shaw. Many ivory stays and busks were made on board for loved ones at home, in much the same spirit as the Welsh love spoons—except that these hardy sailors were often away from home for three or four years. In addition, numerous household and ship-board utensils were made, including rolling-pins, pastry-cutters, clothes-pegs, small boxes, walking-stick handles, cribbage-boards and fids. The tools used in this work were often of the simplest kind, though it is known that the ship's carpenter or blacksmith would occasionally make a lathe or some tool more elaborate than a knife.

The tooth of the sperm whale remained a firm favourite for scrimshaw, but the teeth of other species, such as the right or bowhead whale of the Pacific, were also used. The whalers also made objects from other parts of these great mammals, such as the jaw-bone of the sperm whale and, in particular, the palate of the bowhead whale which produced the remarkable, horn-like substance known as baleen.

In the Hull Museum there is a walrus ivory snuff-box dated 1665, but this may not have been made on board ship, and therefore may not be regarded as scrimshaw. The earliest dated American pieces are the two engraved whale teeth made on board the *Susan of Nantucket* in 1829 (one example is in the Nantucket Historical Association, the other is in the American Museum in Britain, in Bath). There is a lengthy reference to scrimshaw in Herman Melville's *Moby Dick*:

> Throughout the Pacific, and also in Nantucket and New Bedford, and Sag Harbour, you will come across lively sketches of whales and whaling scenes, graven by fishermen [=whalers] themselves, on Sperm Whale teeth, or ladies' busks wroght out of the Right Whale bone, and other skrimshander articles, as the whalemen call numerous little ingenious contrivances they elaborately cut of the rough material, in their hours of ocean leisure. Some have little boxes of dentistical-looking implements, specially intended for the skrimshandering business. But, in general, they toil with their jack-knives alone; and with that almost omnipotent tool of the sailor, they will turn you out anything you please in the way of a mariner's fancy.
>
> Long exile from Chrisendom and civilisation inevitably restores a man to that condition in which God placed him, ie. what is called savagery. Your true whale-hunter is as much a savage as an Iroquois. I myself am a savage, owing no allegiance but to the King of the Cannibals; and ready at any moment to rebel against him. Now, one of the peculiar characteristics of the seaman in his domestic hours, is his wonderful patience of industry. An ancient Hawaiian war-club or spear paddle, in its full multiplicity and elaboration of carving, is as great a trophy of human perseverance as a Latin lexicon. For, with but a bit of broken seashell or a shark's tooth, that miraculous intricacy of wooden network has been achieved; and it has cost steady years of steady applilcation. As with the Hawaiian savage, so with the white sailor-savage. With the same marvellous patience, and with the same single shark's tooth, or his one poor jack-knife. He will carve you a bit of bone sculpture, not quite as work-

manlike, but as close packed in its maziness of design as the Greek savage, Achilles shield; and full barbaric spirit and suggestiveness as the prints of that fine old Dutch savage, Albert Durer.[7]

Ship Portraits and Models The Dutch, notably the Van de Veldes, popularised sophisticated marine pictures. Portraits of individual ships, on the other hand, are of a different order. They show less understanding of composition but more understanding of shipbuilding and seamanship, and a great variety of materials were used. They are not bound by the conformities of academic taste, but they have their own, which could be termed heraldic, or even hieratic!

Many of the earliest ship portraits were in fact votive pictures, and most surviving eighteenth-century specimens are Italian. Italian ship portraitists travelled all over the world in the early nineteenth century; one example is Michel Felice Corné, who was born on the island of Elba in about 1752 and moved to America in 1799.

Many paintings were produced by those who sailed on voyages of exploration and discovery. From John White (a freeman of the Painter Stainers' Company of the City of London, who went to Virginia under the auspices of Sir Walter Raleigh) onwards, such expeditions were commonly accompanied by professional artists, some of whom did not survive the rigours of the voyage. The Banks Collection in the British Museum includes many watercolours by the professional artists or botanists who accompanied Captain James Cook on his voyages to the South Seas, and also some by Cook himself.

Amateur oil paintings on canvas and wood were widespread, and often occur on the inside of the lids of seamen's chests, although it should be noted that fakes abound. The Neapolitan gouache seems to have widely influenced those sailors who dabbled with the brush.

Pictures of ships were occasionally made of cut paper, and at Greenwich there is one dated 1750.

Only seven true glass portraits of ships are known to survive from the eighteenth century, and most of these are Italian. By the nineteenth century a number of Silesian glassworkers based in Belgium seem to have made glass paintings, and today about half the surviving nineteenth-century examples are in Belgian collections. Though British subjects are known of this period, it appears that none of these were painted in Britain.

Woolwork pictures of ships seem to have been almost exclusively the pastime of British seamen. Most specimens seem to show naval ships, so it is possible that they were a particular favourite in the Royal Navy. This seems a fitting place to mention the woolwork pincushions which were

Above: *Sailor's woolwork picture in contemporary frame,*
c1875. Note the paddle steamer at bottom right. 32in by
21½in.
Right: *Detail from a sailor's painting of the* Sea Horse, *a*
fully rigged ship. Oil on canvas, 1820–50, 36in x 25in.

made on board ship as offerings to loved ones at home. The
cushions were usually heart-shaped, though crosses are also
known, and into these were pushed pins with decorative
heads, making patterns and spelling out words. In the late
nineteenth century, photographs were incorporated in these
confections.

Many models were made in the shipyards, for the client
to see and for the shipwrights to work from. Another class
of model was made by the sailors themselves, most famous

threads were pulled, raising the masts, and the bottle was sealed with a cork and sealing-wax. Occasionally objects other than ships—buildings, for example—were made by sailors and placed in bottles in this way, but the ship remained the favourite subject.

These models were not always of the 'ship in a bottle' type. Some sailors' ship models were placed in glass-fronted boxes with a painted backdrop. Most of these are virtually high reliefs, with sails carved of wood or some such solid substance painted white, but some are truly three-dimensional.

1 *Select Naval Documents*, ed. Hodges and Hughes, Cambridge, 1922, page 34.
2 Philip Cowburn, *The Decorative Arts of the Mariner*.
3 *Hogarth Moralized,* London, 1767.
4 Description of the Merchant Taylors' 1764 state barge, quoted in Cowburn (see 2 above).
5 William Sutherland, *The Ship Builder's Assistant*, London, 1711.
6 J. T. Smith, *Nollekens and his Times*, 1919 ed., vol. 1, page 871. The shell-work described here does not sound sufficiently elaborate to be considered as cameo work.
7 Herman Melville, *Moby Dick*.

among them the 'ship in a bottle'. These generally date from the mid-nineteenth century, when glass bottles began to be mass produced. The model was passed through the neck of the bottle, with the masts and spars lying horizontally on the deck pointing aft, the sails of flexible thin paper. The rigging, all of fine thread, was passed over the bowsprit and out of the neck of the bottle. Once the model ship was inside the bottle and floating on a sea of painted putty, the

Left: Pincushion decorated with fancy pins pushed into it, similar to those made by sailors for loved ones at home.
Below: A ship in a bottle made by a sailor.
Right: Woolwork picture of HMS Queen, Malta, May 24th 1851, in contemporary cross-banded mahogany frame. The 24th of May was Queen Victoria's birthday and Empire Day, which probably accounts for the ship's being 'dressed overall'. 29in x 35½in.

The Pictorial Arts

Oil painting is only one element of the wide range of British folk art. Much work was done by the professional, non-academic artist, but the amateur must not be forgotten. Above all, these folk artists employed many materials other than paint in the making of pictures.

The manuals that were published concerning craft methods and materials sometimes included advice for amateurs and others about drawing. In addition, books were published that were exclusively or primarily concerned with such subjects as perspective, miniature painting and ornament, together with pattern-books for the copyist. Robert Sayer's *The Ladies Amusement* is an example of the latter. The rich diversity of these books may be glimpsed by consulting the advertisements for 'Ornaments and Household Furniture' that appeared in *12 Designs for Farm-Houses* by William Halfpenny, Carpenter and Architect (London 1751). A couple of titles listed in this advertisement are as follows:

> A new Book of Ornaments designed for Tablets and Friezes for Chimney-Pieces, useful for Youth to draw after, elegantly engraved on six large Folio Copper Plates, in Imitation of *Chalk*, price 3s. NB. This Book may be had printed either in Red or Black, by Thomas Johnson, Carver.

> A Book containing such Beasts as are most usual for such as practice Drawing, Engraving Coats of Arms, Painting, Chasing, and several other Occasions, designed by Francis Barlow and engraved by William Vaughan.

William Halfpenny himself ventured to produce such a book dealing with that aspect of drawing that fascinates and frustrates so many amateurs. His *Perspective Made Easy*

Left: *Embossed relief paper picture*, The Mock Bird, c1780, 9½in x 11½in.

Right: *Plate 12 from* Twelve Designs for Farmhouses *by William Halfpenny, depicting 'A plan and Elevation for the County of Oxon &c.' London 1774.*

(London 1731) purported to demonstrate 'a new method for Practical Perspective shewing the Use of New-Invented Senographical Protractor; so easy, that a Person, tho' an intire Stranger to Perspective, may, by reading a few Lines, become Master of the Instrument, without the help of a Master.' Whatever the 'Senographical Protractor' may have been there can be no doubt that the camera obscura was generally used to 'take' those prospects where perspective drawing was needed. In the eighteenth century these were stocked by opticians but Dossie[1] describes how to make a camera obscura at home:

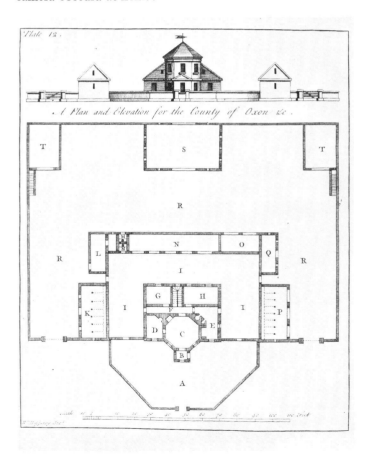

Where they [the camera obscura] are not to hand, and a prospect through any particular window is desired to be taken, an occasional camera may be formed. This is done by boring a hole through a window shutter . . . and putting one of the glasses called the ox-eye, into the hole; when all other light being shut out, except what passes through this hole, and a proper ground of paper vellum etc. being held at a due distance from the hole, the reflected image of the prospect will be formed upon the ground.

He warns, however, that

. . . there is one very material objection to its use. This is, that the shadows lose their force in the reflected image; and objects, by the refraction, are made to appear rounder, or different sometimes both in their magnitude and site, from what they really are, which being oppugnant to the truth of any drawing, allmost wholly destroys the expedience there would be otherwise found in this manner.

Thomas Bardwell, Painter, in *The Practice of Painting*, 1756, goes so far as to say that 'A Painter is not to be confined strictly to the Rules of Perspective but to make them subservient to his purposes.' This sensible advice has been followed by many, especially the folk artists.

Cut Paper

The instruction manuals of the seventeenth century and later include certain artistic crafts which were considered suitable for women of the leisured classes. The art of making wax flowers was widely practised by amateurs as early as the seventeenth century, and by the eighteenth century rolled paper or vellum was used to create gilded and painted pictorial reliefs behind glass. These various creations sometimes provided backplates for sconces, mirror frames and the sides of tea caddies. In 1809 when Mary Howitt was writing of her childhood at a Quaker school in Croydon she described one of these parlour pastimes' or 'mock arts':

We soon furnished ourselves with coloured paper for plaiting and straw to split and weave into net . . . and I shall never forget my admiration of a pattern of diamonds woven of strips of gold paper on a black ground. It was my first attempt to do artistic needlework.[2]

The 'Pin Prickt' picture seems to have been exclusively a young ladies' pastime, and particularly popular in Roman

Catholic schools: many of the subjects are religious. The pricking of the paper produces a relief with a texture that can be varied according to the size of the needle or pin; sometimes a toothed wheel was used to cover larger areas. Details such as faces and hands were usually rendered in watercolour, a feature of some silk embroideries of a similar style. It is possible that such embroidery on paper is the origin of this technique, which might be described as embroidery without thread. On the other hand, the practice of pricking designs through paper for pouncing a design through on to another surface is a more likely source. This type of work is described in *The Young Ladies' Book: a Manual of Elegant Recreations, Exercises, and Pursuits*,[3] where it is recommended that 'the whole of the background or body of the paper [should be] painted in some somber opaque colour to throw up the figure'. The craft is described as 'Piercing Costumes on Paper' and the book suggests as subject matter 'Turkish or other figures in oriental costume or draperies'. Cowper's lines on 'The Receipt of my Mother's Picture' could be referring to this pastime:

Could Time, his flight reversed, restore the hours
When, playing with thy vestures' tissued flowers,
The violets, the pink, the jessamin,
I prick'd them into paper with a pin.

The silhouette was the source of livelihood to many professional artists providing cheap portraits before the intro-

Left: *19th century pinprick and watercolour picture of a boy leading a blind man; 11in x 8in.*
Above: *Late 19th century amateur silhouette of a Farmyard Scene.*
Right: Hunters, *a mid-19th century amateur silhouette.*

duction of photography. It was particularly popular between 1810 and 1840. Some were cut by amateurs. The profile view was certainly more easily rendered by the amateur as *The Miniature Painter's Manual*[4] makes quite clear:

> In commencing the study of drawing from life, the learner will find it advisable to draw the profile of the face, selecting a sitter with a stongly-marked angular countenance [for only then could] the student . . . . proceed to draw the whole face. This will be found to require greater attention . . .

Many examples survive that include certain details of background or dress picked out in watercolour. Cut paper was also the medium for many Valentine cards.

While on the subject of paper, passing reference should be made to the embossed pictures of birds and flowers that are usually attributed to Dixon of Dublin. The paper for these pictures was presumably embossed in an edition in a mould or die of wood with a maximum relief of about 3/8 inch. They were then painted in watercolour by hand and the surviving examples are very elaborate in an idiom slightly reminiscent of chinoiserie. They are usually found in their original frames, which were designed to accommodate the relief, and some of them retain their descriptive labels on the back, for example *The Peacock Pheasant from China, The Pea-Hen Pheasant from China* and *The Mock*

Bird 'brought from Jamaica and in the Possession of T. White of Lincolns Inn, Esq.' These particular examples are often attributed to Dixon but they were in fact 'Sold by Appointment of the Maker H. Baker at R. Williamson's

Bookseller and Printer, near the Exchange in Liverpool'. Although not in the category of high art such pictures still adorn houses of the importance of the Queen's House at Kew, and were thus conceived as 'furnishing' pictures for the nobility.

Collage

Cloth, straw, seeds and shells are only some of the many materials used for collage. Some of the resulting work is in high relief and much of it was by amateurs. The watercolour painting illustrated on page 84 is in fact a collage. The landscape is painted on a sheet of paper but all the dogs, horses and riders are cut out in paper and stuck down. The device enabled the artist to decide on the composition after the painting was complete—a useful ploy for the amateur.

In Britain it is exceptional to find a group of works of folk art by a known individual, but such a person is George Smart of 'Frant, near Tonbridge Wells, Kent, Artist in Cloth and Velvet figures to his Royal Highness the Duke of Sussex'. His pictures, of which a considerable number survive, consist of watercolour drawings forming a background to the stuck-on cloth of which the figures are composed. In some instances an attempt has been made to give form to the relief thus created. Smart may have been exaggerating the importance of his Royal patronage but it is interesting that a personage like the Duke of Sussex (1773–1843) who, unconventional for his time, with pronounced liberal views and a deep interest in the arts, should occasionally have purchased such pictures, even though they may have been relegated to the staff quarters. In *Clifford's Guide to Tunbridge Wells* (Tunbridge Wells 1822 with later editions up to 1851) may be found the following:

> The company from the Wells, in their rides through Frant, are agreeably attracted on entering the village by the *nouvelle* Exhibition of a tailor, who, out of cloth of divers colours, delineates animals and birds of various descriptions, with a variety of grotesque characters, particularly old Bright, the Postman, many years sweeper of Tunbridge Wells Walks, which is considered a good likeness. He has many visitors to inspect this singular collection, who seldom leave his house without becoming purchasers. He calls himself 'Artist in Cloth and Velvet Figures to His Royal Highness the Duke of Sussex', who with his characteristic good humour, patronizes the humble *tailor*. He is not a little proud of his *royal* patronage, which, with the following lines, penned by the village bard, he never forgets to place at the back of ingenious productions.

Another guide to the Spa, W. Kidd's *Pocket Companion*, describes this tailor turned artist with amused disdain:

> While at Frant, it would be inexcusable not to visit Mr. Smart, the far famed *taylor*, who, however *humble* his situation in life may appear we consider worthy a very honourable mention in this place. To quote his own words, he is, in addition to his *profession*, 'artist

The Scottish Girl, *a feltwork picture on a watercolour background by George Smart.*

Opposite, above left: *Cut paper picture of a shepherd and shepherdess with their sheep, inscribed on the back: 'Cut by Mrs Jane West Apl. 1838 for Elias Merrick'. 7in x 12in.*

Above right: *Embossed picture of birds 'Sold by Appointment of the Maker, H. Baker', c1780, 8½in x 11in.*

Below: *Watercolour and collage picture of a hunting field, c1850, 32in x 24in.*

in cloth and velvet figures to His Royal Highness the Duke of Sussex'. These figures were admirably executed, more particularly old Bright, the postman many years sweeper of Tunbridge Wells walks. From my judge of Mr. Smart's capabilities as an artist Mr. Smart is a poet, as may be seen from the following, taken, *by permission,* of course, from his album.

The verse illustrated below left then appears, followed by these lines:

The hint thrown out in the last line is generally taken, few persons visiting the place, without providing themselves with a *memento* of this singular, eccentric, but good humoured taylor—we ask his pardon—'artist'.

In at least one example the price is written in ink on the label at the end of the last line, for example £1.0.0 for Smart's 'The Earth Stopper'. The label describes the postman 'As he returns to TUNBRIDGE-WELLS' and to

Below: *This verse, printed by Clifford of Tunbridge Wells, appeared on the back of the frame of many of Smart's pictures; this suggests that they were sold framed.*

make this more real Smart includes some well-known houses in the background of the various versions of this his favourite subject, among them Eridge Castle. The 'Goose Woman' and 'The Postman' were well-known characters in the district. One of Smart's labels is marked apparently in his handwriting alongside the lines about the postman, 'Aged 87'. Smart was known for a number of other pictures and of these his 'Earth Stopper' was the most amusing; it appears to have been based upon a print after Nathan Drake's *The Earth Stopper* by V. Green published in 1767 —'Arthur Wentworth of Bulmer, near Castle Howard, Yorkshire. Aged 75, Earth Stopper to Charles, late Earl of Carlislle'.*

Native wit and creative talent inspired Smart to extend Drake's composition to include a chimney-sweep and his donkey (see illustration comparing two pictures). A handwritten description of this picture, signed G. Smart, reads:

*The original painting by Nathan Drake, the York artist, who flourished from 1751 to 1783, was made for William Tufnell of Nun Monkton Priory, Yorkshire.

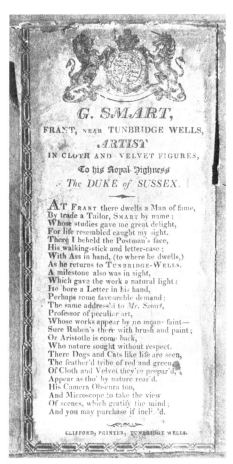

The
EARTH STOPPER

The Business of an Earth Stopper the Night previous to a Day's Sport is to stop up the Fox's Earth whilst he is out Feeding. The above gentle Swain is supposed

Right: Smart's The Earth Stopper, *c1845, one of his well-known feltwork pictures; below it are a more 'mass-produced' example and another which is unfinished. This design is apparently a free adaptation of an engraving of Nathan Drake's painting* The Earth Stopper.

Left and below: Old Bright, The Postman by Smart. The medieval parish church at Frant was rebuilt in the early 19th century – the tower was completed in 1819. Smart's depiction of this in the background is remarkably accurate. These two versions vary in some details: for instance in one the second letter in Bright's hand is addressed to 'The Agent, Mr W . .' while in the other it is in his bag and addressed to 'Mr Lu . .'. The picture on the left is the cruder in execution of the two.

to be on his way home, when by a sudden turn of the Lane he is brought plump upon what he conceives to be nothing more or less than the Dxxxl, but which in fact is a simple Sweep and his Donkey.

[in pencil] £1.0.0

Later versions of the picture by Smart bear this description on a printed label—printed by Clifford of Tunbridge Wells, the same Clifford who published the *Guide*.

The Museum of Royal Tunbridge Wells has a good collection of Smart's work. One picture includes a Hussar who can be made to lift his headdress in salutation; the background shows the estuary of the Medway.[5] The collection also includes a lithograph of Elizabeth Horne at the age of 88 in 1830 by C. Hulton. She was apparently the model for Smart's *The Goosewoman*. Also preserved in the same collection is the following verse on Smart:

IMPROMPTU TO THE INGENIOUS MAKER OF CLOTH AND VELVET FIGURES OF FRANT, NR. TUNBRIDGE WELLS

Come here, I say, come here ye quizzers
Who laugh at Taylors and at scissors,
And see how *Smart* makes that utensil
Out-do the Chisel, Brush and Pencil.
With Genius Quick, and tune to Nature,
He makes a suit for every creature;
And fits alike the whole creation,
In newest style the latest Fashion.
Illustrious *Smart!* Why stayed thou here
Like Violet in the Desert Sir?
Hide not thy modest merit thus
Nor Fame that is thy right refuse.
To the great city haste away,
There give they genius scope and play.
In Glory's circle claim thy entry,
And vie with *Lawrence, Shee,* or *Chantry.*

Smart's pictures made in the second quarter of the nineteenth century were fundamentally watercolours with a collage of various cloths, after the manner of the dressed pictures popular from the late seventeenth century.[6] This type of work became particularly popular in the nineteenth century. A pair of high reliefs in felt in the Judkyn Collection were 'Made by Miss Gimbler/AD 1865'. The same collection also includes a number of what look like conventional sporting prints. Closer inspection reveals that they are in fact pictures composed entirely of felt with the details drawn in with black Indian ink.

Straw-work goes back to our earliest history and the celebration of the harvest. Corn dollies were traditionally made from the last stook to be harvested on a farm . In the nineteenth century Luton was a great centre for lace-making and straw plaiting, along with Stilton and Yaxley and also, according to Arthur Young, writing in 1768, Dunstable. Apart from its fine collection of straw hats, Luton Museum contains a pair of nineteenth-century straw-work dolls

Below, left: *Smart feltwork picture of a Hussar with the River Medway in the background.*

Centre: *Smart's* The Goosewoman.

Right: *Lithograph of Elizabeth Horne, aged 88, published in Tunbridge Wells in June 1830. This is thought to have been Smart's model for* The Goosewoman.

Top: *Feltwork relief of contemporary figures made by Miss Gimbler, 1865, 18in x 25in.*

Above: *One of a series of four feltwork sporting pictures, Hare Coursing, in maplewood frame, c1835, 22in x 17in.*

Right: *Two straw work dolls with wax faces; the round wooden base suggests that they were originally placed under a glass dome.*

fashionably dressed in clothes made entirely of straw, although their faces are of wax.

The French prisoners held in Britain during the Napoleonic Wars were renowned for their ivory ship models and dominoes and for their straw marquetry. Sometimes these skills were combined, the bone and ivory ship model being enclosed in a glazed case constructed of wood decorated with straw-work. For this purpose the straw—of different

degrees of ripeness to provide a range of colours and tones —was split with a sharp knife and then ironed flat; it could then be used simply as veneer. Peterborough Museum has a fine collection of this work from the nearby camp at Norman Cross. A group of Welsh straw-work pictures of the mid-nineteenth century appear to be the work of one person, as the landscapes and portraits of houses are identified on these pictures in the same hand. Like Smart's work, they are combined with watercolour.

The immortelle was not only a popular part of the Victorian way of death, but also provided an embellishment in the home for the Victorian way of life. These were made commercially of wax but amateurs used silk, cloth and shells, out of which they constructed flowers. *Dickens's Dictionary of London,* 1879, lists under 'Tradesmen' to Queen Victoria 'WAX FLOWERS, MODELLER OF. — Mintorn, J. H. 33, Soho-sq'. When complete, these com-

positions were embalmed under glass. Such confections of rolled paper, shells, straw, seeds, felt and wax were also made in the eighteenth century when they were usually two-dimensional and placed in picture-frames, the outside section of some of which suggesting that they were intended to be set into a wall. These works have a curious *trompe-l'oeil* quality—are they pictures of objects, or are they objects in themselves?

Drawing

Many old manuals contain instructions on drawing and the materials that may be used. The *Polygraphice*[7] states that 'The Instruments of Drawing are Sevenfold, viz. Charcoals, Feathers of a Ducks Wing, Black and Red Lead Pencils,

Far left, above: *Welsh straw work picture of the Menai Straits.*

Far left, below: *Wooden glazed box containing a scene of an old man and woman sitting outside their cottage; made entirely of flower and vegetable seeds; 7in x 5½in x 2in, c1800.*

Left: *A pair of shellwork bouquets in vases c1860, 15in high.*

Below: *Saltwood Church and Castle from a sketch book of Arthur Vine Hall (1824–1919).*

Pens made of Ravens Quills, Rulers, Compasses, Pastels, or Crions' and goes on 'Observe to draw all your Out-lines at first very faint . . . because, if amis, you may rub them out with the Feathers of a Duck's wing, or a bit of Bread . . .' Even as late as 1876 Gwilt's *Encyclopaedia of Architecture* includes a chapter on drawing[8] which bears comparison with the eighteenth century:

> The learner is usually first put to copying drawings or prints . . . *Outline** is the foundation of all drawing; the alphabet of graphic art . . . in general a year of steady application may be sufficient . . . after which he ought to be capable of inventing for himself . . .

Often it was the too close observance of such suggestions, their application as rules, that has resulted in some of the oddest and most delightful examples of naïve drawings. However as Gwilt points out, all artists have their naïve moments:

> The majority of men who can draw the figure tolerably well can draw nothing else correctly . . . the representation by our best portrait painters of the accessories which they introduce into their pictures, especially of architectural details, is almost without exception ludicrously inaccurate.

It is generally considered that penmanship gained vitality, especially in America, with the introduction of the steel-nibbed pen in the early nineteenth century. The assumption that calligraphic artists before that time knew only the quill

*The *Encyclopaedia of Architecture* does not omit the question of modelling and devotes a whole section to 'Sciography or the doctrine of shadows . . .'

is in question, for John Ayres, one of the greatest seventeenth-century writing masters, advertised himself in 1680 as 'Master of the Writing School at the 'Hand and Pen' near St Paul's School in St Paul's Church Yard, where Gentlemen may be furnished with the best sorts of Steel Pens'.[9]

Watercolours

'Limning', according to William Salmon,[10] 'is an Art whereby in water Colours, we strive to resemble Nature in everything to the life'. In Salmon's day the word had retained its association specifically with watercolour* but by the nineteenth century the word was obsolete. Today it is fashionably though imprecisely applied to those paintings where the craft element is uppermost.

'Drawling, Stretching and Fainting in Coils' or something close to it was, as Lewis Carroll suggested, an important part of a young girl's education in the first half of the nineteenth century. It is perhaps less well known that it was also an important part of a young gentleman's education. At Sandhurst painting in watercolour was part of a cadet's training. Their work may be said to be that of sophisticated amateurs who, while often displaying considerable dexterity, did not approach the standard of craftsmanship that only years of apprenticeship could achieve. These dilettantes must thus be seen as a group distinct from folk artists in general.

When the Royal Academy was founded in 1768, watercolour painting was not highly regarded. It was thus to some extent left to the amateurs by default and some achieved a

*From 'luminer', one who illuminated manuscripts. Hilliard painted his miniatures in watercolour, and he wrote a pamphlet entitled *The Art of Limning*.

Far left, above: *Interior of a cottage near Bexley Hill, Maidstone, by Arthur Vine Hall*
Far left, below: *Watercolour portrait of a young boy leaning against a giraffe piano. The inscription on the piano reads: 'Routh. Maker 1832'.*
Left: *Three profile portraits, watercolour on paper in contemporary maplewood frames: John Brown aged 9 years, 9th February 1855 (9in x 10in); Betsy Brown (10in x 12in); an elderly woman, possibly their mother (9in x 10in).*

Right: *Watercolour of Charles Norton of the 9th Regiment, c1875, 7in x 5in.*

standard that was later acceptable to the Royal Academy and its Summer Exhibitions. Charlotte Canning (1817–1861) was a competent watercolour painter and according to Ruskin capable of painting 'the grandest representations of flowers' he had ever seen.[11]

Before the days of photography, watercolour painting was used by the armed services as a means of recording enemy positions. A great British photographer, Fenton, recorded the Crimean War (1835–1856) while British officers there painted delightful and sensitive watercolours. This was perhaps the last time that such an activity was seen as an integral part of warfare. (The official war artists of the last war were present for the sake of posterity and not as part of an intelligence service.) During the Peninsular War le Marchant was one of the greatest of the officer artists and his last picture, painted on the eve of the battle in which he fell, is still in the possession of the family. At Woolwich, the chief drawing-master was for a while Paul Sandby. The British army officer was therefore trained at

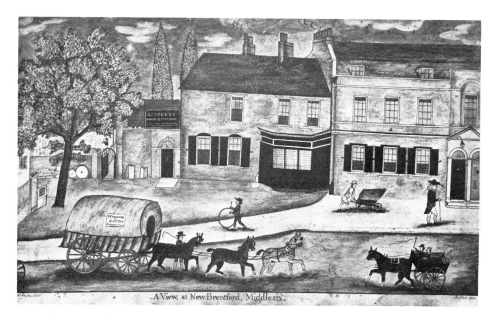

a professional level as a mature man, and much of this work falls outside the purview of this book.

The manufacture of watercolour-cakes by Reeves & Son (founded in 1766) did much to encourage watercolour painting. This innovation freed artists from the drudgery of making their own watercolours, using gum arabic as the medium.[12]

Embroidery

After the reformation of the monasteries the home market for elaborately embroidered vestments declined and England lost her pre-eminent reputation for Opus Anglicanum. Embroidery as a trade employing both men and women became an accomplishment for women of the leisured classes. The first samplers, or examplers as they were also known, date from Tudor times. These early pieces are not seen as cohesive pictures but rather as a series of individual exercises on one piece of cloth. The influence of the medieval herbals and bestiaries is evident and also books such as *La Clef des Champs* (published at Blackfriars in 1586) by Jacques le Moyne who is also known for his drawings of Florida engraved by Theodore de Bry. The most important work was, however, Johann Sibmacher's *Schon Modelbuch* published in Nurnberg in 1597—it continued to be published in Germany and the last edition appeared in 1877. It was this influential book that was the source of many of the illustrations in *The Needle's Excellency* by John Taylor published in London in 1632. Copies

Top left: *Watercolour of New Brentford, Middlesix* (sic) inscribed 'H. Sexton Del[t] et fecit 1804'. $16\frac{1}{2}$in x $21\frac{1}{2}$in.
Top right: *A somewhat more accomplished watercolour of a family group. Mid–19th century*, $13\frac{1}{2}$in x $10\frac{1}{2}$in.
Above: *Title page of the 1636 edition of John Taylor's* The Needle's Excellency.

are now rare. Many must have been destroyed when the illustrations were transferred onto fabric by the old method of 'pricking' through the designs and 'pouncing' with charcoal. Another important source of reference was William

Simpson's *The Second Book of Flowers, Fruits, Beasts, Birds and Flies exactly Drawn* (1656), even the title is redolent of a set of crewel bed hangings or a 'stump-work' casket. Many of these books that gave inspiration to the embroiderer were on gardening. Books of this type continued to appear into the eighteenth century—a good example being *The Flower Garden Displayed* by Robert Furber (1732).

Drawing and painting in watercolours together with embroidery were essential social accomplishments for the young lady of good family in the early nineteenth century. In fact something of this attitude has persisted. There was too the emerging Victorian view that idleness was evil, although a verse in *The Needle's Excellency* shows that these attitudes have long been characteristic:

"Here practise and invention may be free
And as the squirrel skips from tree to tree
So maids may (from their mistresse or their mother)
Learn to leave one worke, and learne another.
For here they may make choice of which is which,
and skip from worke to worke, from stitch to stitch,
Until, in time, delightful practise shall
(with profit) make them perfect in them all.
Thus hoping that these workes may have this guide
To serve for ornament, and not pride:
To cherish vertue, banish idleness,
For these ends, may this booke have good successe."

Early samplers—that is to say early seventeenth century ones—are frequently long and narrow in vertical proportion, for example 20 inches by 6 inches. Towards the close of the seventeenth century and in the early eighteenth century samplers became more square, alphabets and verse more common and compositions single units rather than a series of exercises. Many reveal the extreme youth of their makers. A 6 year old Eleanor Sarah Hooper in 1846 embroidered:

Behold the labour of my tender age
And view this work which did my hours engage
With anxious care I did these colours place
A smile to gain from my dear Parents face
Whose care of me I ever will regard
And pray that God will give a kind reward. ·

By the late nineteenth century when samplers were declining in importance a *Dictionary of Needlework* (1882) was quite dogmatic "*To make a sampler*: Cut this Mosaic Canvas 18 inches wide and 20 inches long and measure off a border all round 4 inches". With the tradition frozen the days of the sampler were numbered. In the late eighteenth

Right: Two samplers, by Ann Brasher and Anne Roberts, expressing characteristic sentiments.

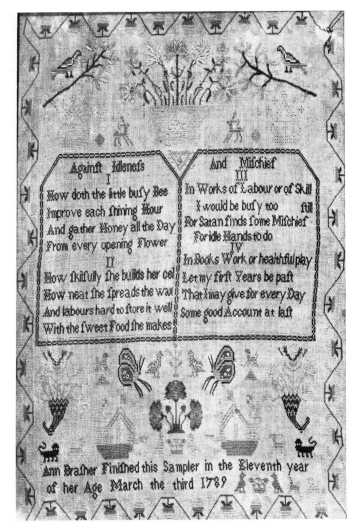

Above left: *Mary J. Heazell's sampler dated 1883.*

Above: *An embroidered picture on silk stitched in silk with long and short stem stitch and split stitch. The details are painted in watercolour.*

Left: Christ Rising from the Tomb: *silkwork picture in a rosewood frame. The faces of the figures are cut out from engravings. 18in x 17in.*

century map samplers make their appearance when other subjects compete for the attentions of the young needle-woman. Among these pictures with religious subject matter were popular, and may be related to the pin prick pictures (see under Cut Paper) that could be described as embroidery without silk. In fact in the years before and after 1800

Right: *Watercolour of Joseph Pestell with his wife and child; the details are picked out in gold and the uniform has sequin buttons.*

Private, Wife and Child

Of Her Majesty's 21st Regiment, Or Royal North British Fusiliers

embroidered pictures on paper or silk were fashionable, with figure subjects, hands and faces were left unembroidered, these details being rendered in watercolour. At this time embroidered pictures and samplers were professionally framed with black glass mounts. In America this type of work is known as Seminary art as much of it was carried out in girls' schools.

Painting without Frames

The archaeological zeal of the Romans took the form of Philhellenism which was the ruling fashion after Marcellus despoiled Syracuse of its principal statues in 212 BC. In turn, Renaissance artists were inspired by the work of ancient Rome. This amounted to more than the influence of the Belvedere Torso on Michelangelo. Figures in marble were made copying those that were found, fragmentary and uncoloured. Most civilizations have been the patrons of both architecture and sculpture (stone and wood) that was coloured (and only an archaeological outlook would find the manufacture of a fragment anything but ludicrous). There are exceptions, for when special materials were used the use of colour was withheld, but even Purbeck marble was coloured towards the end of its period of fashion.

As late as the seventeenth century the use of colour was widespread in England. Celia Fiennes in her *Journeys on a*

Side Saddle in the Reign of William and Mary describes the Jacobean font at Durham as follows: 'The font is of marble, the top carved wood . . . and resembles a picture of the tower of Babel, its not painted . . .' It is significant that in the year 1697 she should remark that the woodwork is not coloured. Even John van Nost (d. 1729) painted his lead garden ornaments. Two of his most popular figures, the kneeling slaves supporting sundials on their heads, described as an 'Indian' and 'Blackamoor', cost £30 each. The examples preserved at Melbourne Hall, Derbyshire, 'have considerable traces of the colouring with which they were painted—black bodies, white eyes, and brightly coloured sashes' and records show that all the ironwork and leadwork at this house was painted at regular intervals; 'for colouring ye urns and 2 large statues: for gilding two flames for ye urns: for colouring ye boys and ye 2 pedistals'.[14]

Generally the use of paint in post-medieval England suggests the continuation of a tradition that the 'higher' culture abandoned. ('High' culture re-adoption of painted work through Robert Adam was the result of more efficient archaelogy and the realisation that even the Romans used painted decoration.) In this sense the carved wood painted shop sign or figurehead may be seen as a survival of pre-Renaissance values.

The painting of carriages with family coats of arms and ciphers provided a living for many artists. Many of these devices were used by families for self-aggrandisement. Richard Steele, writing in *The Tatler*, claims to 'have given directions to all the coachmakers and coach painters in town, to bring me lists of their several customers . . . It is high time, that I call in such coaches as are in their embelishment improper for the character of their owners . . .'[15] According to Sir Walter Scott this work became even more elaborate in the second quarter of the eighteenth century on British stage coaches:

Upon the doors, also, there appeared but little of that gay blazonry which shines forth upon the numerous quadrigae of the present time; but there were in large characters the names of the places whence the coach started, and whither it went, stated in quaint and ancient language.[15]

The craftsmanship that such carriage and coach painting demanded was enormous. The processes were similar for japanning as described by Stalker and Parker: four undercoats of japan and oil, each succeeding coat having less of the former and more of the latter, then many coats of a mixture of powdered vine charcoal, turpentine and japan. Once this surface was hard it was rubbed down with pumice stone and water. Only then could the final coats of the final

colour be applied. The completed work would then have as many as six coats of copal varnish. The final process, polishing, was often undertaken after some months of use when the carriage would be returned to the maker for this finishing touch. The polishing involved the use of abrasives, pumice and rottenstone, followed by rubbing with bare hands, and finally the carriage was polished with flour and sweet oil. Daily or twice daily washing by the carriage groom hardened the surface and also helped to maintain it. The cost of buying and maintaining a carriage was very great. The Royal State Coach designed by Chambers was exceptional but the costings are of interest for the way in which they cast light on the relative costs of different crafts; for example the carver's work cost more than the coachbuilder's:

	£ s d
Coachmaker	1,673.15.0
Carver	2,500. 0.0
Gilder	933.14.0
Painter	315. 0.0
Laceman	737.10.7
Chaser	665. 4.6
Harnessmaker	385.15.0
Mercer	202. 5.10½
Bitt-maker	99. 6.6
Millener	31. 3.4
Sadler	10.16.6
Woolen-draper	4. 3.6
Cover-maker	3. 9.6

£7,562. 4.3½ [16]

Left: *Detail from a watercolour (c1815) by W. Hamlet of the London to Plymouth mail coach, showing the Royal Arms and the initials GR III.*
Above: *Detail from a painting by James Pollard (1797–1859) of a privately owned stage coach on the London, Leicester, Derby and Manchester route outside the Peacock Inn in Islington, dated 1836.*

Many people hired their carriages, and the 'rent-a-carriage' business became a lucrative sideline for the coachbuilder.

Specialist artists painted the lining on carriages using very long-haired brushes. On private carriages the large, bold coat of arms of the eighteenth century gave way in the late nineteenth century to very small and discreet crests or monograms. The Royal Mail stage coach developed a distinctive livery:

> Maroon body panels bearing on each door the Royal Arms in gold, the cypher of the ruling sovereign, 'GR', 'WR', 'VR', as the case may be on the black painted sides of the front boot, on each of the upper panels (on either side of the windows) appeared one of the stars of the four great orders of knighthood of the United Kingdom—the Garter, Bath, Thistle and St Patrick while each mail bore its number on the hind boot and words 'Royal Mail' with the names of its two terminus cities on its road.[17]

Some private coach proprietors had their own livery for stage coaches, such as Edward Sherman's yellow fleet running from his famous Bull and Mouth Inn at St Martins le Grand; among them was the famous Shrewsbury and London express, 'The Wonder'. De Quincy writes of the many 'flash' turnouts that appeared on British roads in the nineteenth century, but by Victorian times black or a discreet maroon were usual.

Many well-known artists were apprenticed to coach painters. These include John Baker RA, Charles Catton RA (both of whom were apprenticed to Maxfield of Norwich), Joshua Kirby and Richard Dalton, and the American Edward Hicks. Edward Edwards was reluctant in his praise of John Baker when he wrote:

> . . . it must be allowed that his productions had considerable merit, although they were too much marked by that sharpness of touch, which is peculiar to all those who have been bred coach painters.[18]

Overmantel Pictures

With the exception of overmantel pictures, folk artists used landscape painting mainly for backgrounds. William Halfpenny's *Perspective Made Easy* (1731) must have been

Right: *Overmantel picture showing the East front of Urchfont Manor (known as Erchfont House until 1767). It is believed to have been based on the architect's drawings, c1690.*
Below: *Overmantel picture painted in oil on a deal panel, 16in x 46in.*

invaluable. This book claimed to be 'Useful in taking the Perspective Draughts of Towns, Countrys, and Gardens or any Objects whatever . . .' Overmantel pictures or panels to contain them have been an important part of interior decoration from the time of Inigo Jones. Batty Langley's *The Builder's and Workman's Treasury of Design* etc. (1750)

contains twenty designs for 'Tabernacle Frames' of which only two are of a horizontal proportion and both are attributed to Inigo Jones. In America such pictures were nearly always of this proportion as the larger, wood-burning fires and lower ceilings left little room above the mantel piece. In England, however, coal-burning fireplaces and higher ceilings resulted in overmantel pictures of a square shape. Removed from their context, the original use of these pictures can be difficult to identify although the 'fielded panel' is often a clue. Overmantel pictures of a surprisingly primitive sort, although never found in the houses of the nobility, may be seen in the homes of the gentry. Urchfont Manor in Wiltshire has an almost complete series showing the house and its grounds as a naïve continental garden.

Landscape painted on glass, mid–19th century.

Glass Painting

Although glass painting (as distinct from painted fired glass for windows) was a well-established art form in the middle ages* it was not at all common in the post-medieval world. Stalker and Parker in their *Treatise on Japaning*, published in 1688, give lengthy 'Directions in Painting Mezzotinto-Prints' and instructions on how 'To lay Prints on Glass'. No mention is made of glass painting as such. Perhaps, as a consequence, transfer prints on glass are quite common but though the colouring is often vigorous to the extent of being primitive the mezzotints that were used in this pastime have all the languid sophistication of their period.

As has been seen, certain foreign artists—mainly Italian and Central European—painted shipping pictures on glass, but this does not seem to have been a British art form. Some seventeenth-century Dutch paintings on glass are known, the most spectacular being those where the recession of a landscape is achieved on three or more layers of glass. This idea was in fact adopted by Gainsborough who used a series of illuminated painted glass plates to form a peepshow which he used in the composition of landscapes. (The original is in the Victoria and Albert Museum). John Smith in *A Short and Direct Method of Painting in Water-Colours* (1730) describes a 'Manner of Painting Window-transparences'. In the early nineteenth century the upper panel of some pier and other mirror glasses was painted in the 'eglomisé' technique. In the eighteenth century Vauxhall

Right:
Oil painting on canvas, Orpheus Charming the Birds and Beasts, *c1700, 48in x 32in.*

mirror glass was exported to China, painted and returned to Europe. All the above examples of glass painting belong to the high culture of their time.

Around the middle of the nineteenth century a certain type of standardised landscape back-painted on glass was popular. These pictures nearly always measure about 2 ft by 1 ft 4 in and include in the composition a cloudy blue sky, feathery trees, some water (river or lake with perhaps a boat), a castle, a cottage and a figure. The character of the castle is often as foreign looking as those that appear on narrow boats and it is possible that these glass pictures were made by German craftsmen resident in England; they may even have been imported. The frames are either of birds-eye maple with 'German gold'* slips, or of the simplest 'composition'†. The standardisation of framing, dimension and composition, and above all the evident speed with which these pictures were painted, suggests that they were mass produced. In at least one known instance the central portion of one of these compositions has been scraped away and a delightful farmyard scene introduced.

*In the Victoria and Albert Museum there is an example of a Flemish Crucifixion, back-painted in distemper on glass, c. 1500. (4473—1858).

*German gold was a means of applying with hot rollers 'metal' or non-precious metal to wood for picture frames and is commonly seen in framing of the second half of the nineteenth century.
†A type of gesso used for cast as opposed to carved ornament.

Easel Painting & Portraits

In high society there was in the eighteenth century an attempt to draw up rules on the areas where different sorts of pictures could, with propriety, be hung. William Salmon[19] gives the following advice:

Of Disposing of Pictures and Paintings . . .

III   Let the *Porch* or entrance into the house be set out with *Rustic* figures, and things rural.

IV   Let the *Hall* be adorned with Shepherds, Peasants, Milk-maids, Neat-herds, Flocks of Sheep and the like, in their respective places and proper attendants; as also Fowls, Fish, and the like.

V   Let the *Stair-case* be set with some admirable monument or building, wither new or ruinous, to be seen and observed at a view passing up: and let the Ceiling over the top of the Stair be put with figures foreshortened looking downward out of Clouds, with Garlands and Cornucopias.

VI   Let Landskips, Hunting, Fishing, Fowling, Historics, and Antiquities be put in the Great *Chamber.*

VII   In the *Dining Room* let be placed the Pictures of the King and Queen or their Coat of Arms.

VIII   Upon *Chimney*-pieces etc etc put only Landskips.

IX   In *Banqueting-Rooms* put cheerful and merry Paintings as of Baccus, Centaures, Satyres, Syrens, and the like but forebearing all obscene Pictures.

It is difficult to say to what extent early eighteenth-century interior decoration obeyed this catechism but such a list makes clear the wide diversity of subject matter used by the

painter, and most of these subjects were attempted by folk artists.

Portraiture in general is a great feature of American work of this nature but it is rather uncommon in England. American art historians have established that a number of British-born folk painters worked in America, among them John Hazlitt, a portrait and miniature artist, brother of the writer William, who lived in New York and Massachusetts from 1783 to 1787.[20] Perhaps where vanity was concerned a greater effort was made to commission sophisticated work which in turn encouraged more academic portrait painting—provincial it often was, but unsophisticated seldom. Furthermore, many painters of national repute worked in the provinces.

In contrast to those painters of human portraits were those who represented on canvas a prize bull or a remarkable sheep. Here the standards were not dynastic and artistic but concerned breeding and agricultural values. In some instances such animal pictures look like architectural elevations of something designed and drawn but not built: an aspiration rather than an achievement. Such a beast is represented by W. Bagsh(aw?) of 'Rougby', a most improbable looking *White Ram* which the artist has by way of reassurance inscribed 'Bred and Fed by R. Smith 1846'.

Those artists that specialised in sporting painting tended to occupy a rather lowly status. Edward Edwards in *Anecdotes of Painters*, 1808, dismisses Roper as being of little consequence: 'His powers as an artist were not considerable, yet sufficient to satisfy the gentlemen of the turf and stable.' While the portraits of animals display anatomical detail with pride, the portraits of people tend to stress either the elegance of the personage as symbolised by surrounding possessions, or the trade or occupation of the sitter.

Professional painters producing unconsciously naïve portraits were most active in the days before the introduction of daguerreotype in 1839. Some were house painters such as George Evans who 'Practised as a house painter, but frequently painted portraits . . . Much cannot be said of his powers as an artist, nor will his portraits be much in request with posterity'.[21]

The great John Kay of Edinburgh (1742–1826), barber, miniaturist, and through his engraved cartoons social commentator, is a rare instance of a British folk portraitist about whom a fair amount is known.[20] He was born in April 1742 in a tenement house known as 'Gibraltar', a little to the

Above left: *Oil painting on canvas, c1865, 18in x 16in.*
Left: *Oil painting on canvas, early 19th century. The cow is probably a Dexter.*

Above: *Leith Volunteer, a portrait of William Grinly etched by John Kay in 1795.*
Right: *Still life in oil on canvas with a maplewood frame. Signed and dated on the back 'M. B. Higginson 1869 – painted Madely, Staffordshire'. Notice the decorated cheese cradle.*

south of Dalkeith. His father, a mason by trade, died in 1748 and John was sent to live with relatives at Leith (now part of Edinburgh), while another brother is said to have emigrated to America. At the age of thirteen he was apprenticed to a Dalkeith barber named George Heriot, and when he had served his time moved to central Edinburgh working as a journeyman barber for seven or nine years. By 1771 he was able to set up in business for himself. The social status of a barber at this time was quite high. One of his clients, Mr William Nisbet, became a patron of Kay, first as barber, then as artist. They became firm friends and, according to Kay's second wife, Nisbet 'at last became so fond of him that for several years before he died particularly the last two he had him almost constantly with him by night and by day'. Nisbet, the owner of a fine estate, was aware that not only was the first Mrs Kay deprived of her husband's company, she was also deprived of his earnings; accordingly he sent her money regularly. After Nisbet's death in 1784 Kay received an allowance from the family and was thus released from the necessity of working as a barber. It was in late 1787 that Kay, two years a widower, married Margaret Scott (d. 1835) who recorded much of what is known of her husband's life. 'He cared for no employment except that of etching likenesses'. For these he charged one guinea for the first 'pull' and half a guinea for subsequent impressions. He may have painted an occasional inn sign—certainly one of his engravings is based on the favourite sign, The Five Alls. His prints, which are outside the scope of this book, placed his reputation at a national level; it is known that he visited London in 1800. On the other hand, Kay's surviving paintings, which include two self portraits, are of great interest. Robert Chambers, in the *Biographical Dictionary of Eminent Scotsmen*, dismissed Kay on the grounds that 'Being entirely self-taught, Kay's work is of negligible artistic merit.' Dickens describes the work of Miss la Creevy, an artist such as Kay, in *Nicholas Nickleby*:

> . . . two portraits in naval dress coats with faces looking out of them and telescopes attached; one of a young gentleman in a very vermilion uniform, flourishing a

sabre; and one of a literary character with a high forehead, a pen and ink, six books, and a curtain. There was, moreover, a touching representation of a young lady reading a manuscript in an unfathomable forest, and a charming whole length of a large-headed little boy, sitting on a stool with his legs fore-shortened to the size of salt-spoons. Besides these works of art, there were a great many heads of old ladies and gentlemen smirking at each other out of blue and brown skies . . .

While inanimate objects are often represented by these artists with loving care as backgrounds for animated compositions of people and animals, the still life seems to be a comparatively rare choice. M. B. Higginson's *Cheshire Cheese, Loaf of Bread and Bottle of Wine*, is unusual in this respect though overmantel pictures sometimes use this type of decorative convention.

FRAMING

More fine pictures have survived than fine frames, for many of the greatest picture collections of Britain were re-framed in the nineteenth century and the old frames burnt in order to recover the gold. The replacement frames were of 'composition' (cast gesso), which imitated the carved work. Grand pictures for stately houses, painted by fashionable artists, were placed in frames made by professional framers.

The folk artists on the other hand, regarded the frame as part of their responsibility and often made their own. In some instances the frame had to be designed to accommodate a particular creation. It was for this reason that 'shadow boxes', a type of frame consisting of a glass-fronted box, were made. At other times convention ruled the choice:

> Your Frames for glass-painting are usually made of stained Pear tree, with narrow mouldings for little pieces, which increase in breadth, as the size of your picture does in largness; they are made with Rabets, and are afforded for 6, 8, and 12 pence, or more according to their dimensions.*

Frames of this type, today known as 'Hogarth' frames, were however also used to frame prints.

Rosewood frames were popular in the first half of the nineteenth century but by the second half, composition frames were used with tedious regularity. Nevertheless birds-eye maple† was popular with frames that were either

*By glass-painting Stalker and Parker here refer to transfer prints painted on glass.
†Nina Fletcher Little informs me that this was so rarely used in America for framing that it may point to the English origin of a picture.

flat or moulded in section. Occasionally a simulated maple frame is found, and cross-banded mahogany frames were also popular at about this time .

Note It is extraordinary how little attention has been given to the subject of framing. Books on antiques omit it while writers on artists to whom the frame was an important element of their work (for example, Italian primitives and American naïve artists like Hicks), are often subjected to the whim of an art editor who with no reason and less taste will crop the frame from an illustration.

1   Robert Dossie, *The Handmaid to the Arts*, London, 1764, page 394.
2   Quoted by Margaret Lambert and Enid Marx, *English Popular Art*, London, 1951, page 51.
3   See also E. D. Longman and S. Loch, *Pins and Pincushions*, London, 1911.
4   Nathaniel Whittock, *The Miniature Painter's Manual*, London, 1844, chapter II.
5   See article by R. F. Johnson in *Country Life*, 15 September 1960.
6   *Antiques* magazine (USA), December 1963, pages 694–7.
7   William Salmon, *Polygraphice*, book I, chapter II.
8   Gwilt, *Encyclopaedia of Architecture*, new ed. London, 1876, 1876, vol. I, chapter IV, page 762.
9   Ambrose Heal, *The English Writing-Masters and their Copy Books 1570–1800*, Cambridge, 1931.
10 William Salmon (see 7 above), book II, chapter XV.
11 Virginia Surtees, *Charlotte Canning*, London, 1975.
12 See John Smith, *A Short and Direct Method of Painting in Water-colours*, London, 1730.
13 A. Lady, *The Young Lady's Friend, A Manual of Practical Advice and Instruction*, London, 4th edn., 1841.
14 Quoted by Christopher Hussey, *English Gardens and Landscapes 1700–1750*, London, 1967, page 62.
15 Quoted by Ralph Straus, *Carriages and Coaches*, London, 1912.
16 Hugh McCausland, *The English Carriage*, London, 1948, page 113.
17 Edward Edwards, *Anecdotes of Painters*, London, 1808.
18 William Salmon (see 7 above), book III, chapter 15.
19 See N. F. Little, *American Decorative Wall Painting*.
20 Hilary and Mary Evans, *John Kay of Edinburgh*, Aberdeen, 1973.

Right: Alfred Openshaw, born July 1846, *oil on canvas by R. Hunt, 36in x 30in.*
Over page: Champion Bull and Prize Cabbage, *oil on board, 14½in x 33½in. The treatment of the figures as isolated profiles is typical of folk art. The picture is signed 'W. Williams 1804'.*

Inside the Home

Interior decoration would be too grand a term to describe the embellishment of the rooms inside a farmhouse or cottage. It is an area that has been little studied.

Wall Decoration

The external wall paintings of Austria and Bavaria have no equivalent in England. However, pargeting, a type of

Left: *Watercolour* The Drawing Room, c1840. *Such work by middle class amateurs provides valuable information on the interior decoration of their homes.*
Below: *Two houses decorated with pargeting in Clare, Suffolk: Church House and a house in Nethergate Street.*

plaster relief decoration, was common from London to East Anglia up to the seventeenth century, but this was essentially monochromatic decoration. Sometimes in the eighteenth and early nineteenth centuries a blind or blocked-up window would have a *trompe l'oeil* window painted in, often on a Welsh slate ground. There is an example in Bath which even includes a blind partly pulled down with a tassel, all painted with loving naturalism.

In important households the use of tapestry, panelling and wall painting for interiors continued well into the seventeenth century. By the eighteenth century the introduction of wallpaper resulted in a decline in the earlier wall treatments. It was the very grand houses, such as Blenheim Palace, and the very much humbler ones, that continued to use murals. An example of the latter is an eighteenth-century wall painting in the George Inn at

Chesham, Buckinghamshire. Paintings of this type and date are extremely rare in England. At a higher social level it is equally rare to find examples of seventeenth-century panelling which retain their original colour, such as that described in the 1649 inventory of Wimbledon Hall which was multicoloured in contrast to the late seventeenth- and early eighteenth-century practice of painting panelling white with gold enrichments.[1] The Painted Room at Wilsley House, Cranbrook, Kent, is an exception. In a somewhat primitive manner it shows on the panels of the dado hounds chasing a rabbit while the panels above are painted with ships at sea. Painting of this sort relates to that of overmantel pictures.

Stalker and Parker allude with some displeasure to yet another form of painted panelling:

> Before Japan was made in England, the imitation of Tortoiseshell was much in request, for Cabinets, Tables, and the like; but being greedy of Novelty, made these give way to modern inventions: not, but that tis still in vogue, and fancied by many for glass-frames, and small Boxes; nay House-Painters have of late frequently endeavoured it, for Battens, and Mouldings of Rooms.[2]

Apparently the best tortoiseshell effects could be achieved on a 'silver foil' ground laid upon a smooth-grained wood like pear tree, or a coarse-grained wood like oak or deal, or a gesso ground. A gesso ground was also demanded to simulate, on wood panelling, white marble with black veins. The black was derived from 'Vines burnt and grinded'. It was then necessary to 'flush or lay the faintest large clouds and veins of your Marble, which being laid on whilst the work is wet, will lie so soft and sweet, that the original will not exceed it . . . Lastly, take a small-pointed feather, and with the deepest colour touch and break all your suddain or smaller veins . . .'

Occasionally eighteenth-century woodwork was 'grained' but this practice did not become widespread until the nineteenth century. Loudon in his *Cottage, Farm and Villa Architecture* (first published in 1836) states that:

> All woodwork avowed as such, should, if possible, be grained in imitation of some natural wood; not with a view of having the imitation mistaken for the original, but rather to create allusion to it, and, by a diversity of lines and shades, to produce a kind of variety and

Above left: *Painted wall decoration in an upstairs room at the George Inn, Chesham, Buckinghamshire.*

Left: *Painted panel decoration bearing the date 1618 from Bennett's Castle Farm House, Dagenham, Essex. The building was demolished in 1938.*

106

intricacy, which affords more pleasure to the eye than a flat shade of colour.

The methods for doing this work were fully described in Smith's *Art of House-Painting*, (revised by Butcher, London 1825). To 'create an allusion' may have been the intention of some of this interior paintwork but others undoubtedly attempted to produce an illusion. Thomas Corbett mentions a grotto near Clifton, Bristol, where 'in this . . . *art* out-does all common art; for here is a door and stair-case *painted!* to make some amends for the want of a real one.' J. T. Smith writes:

> Capitsoldi upon his arrival, took the attic storey of a house in Warwick Street, Golden Square [London], and being short of furniture, painted chairs, pictures, and window-curtains, upon the walls of his sitting room, most admirably deceptive . . .[3]

Overmantel pictures have already been considered but it should be stressed that on occasion each panel in a panelled room would be painted with a decorative landscape or some such composition. A George II room at the Manor Farm, Hughenden, contains a particularly successful example. Here the panels of the dado contain complete individual landscapes while the landscapes of the larger upper panels may be 'read' as individual compositions or as a continuous landscape. Painting direct on plaster was also practised in eighteenth-century England, though lamentably few examples survive. The example found in a small room in the George Inn (formerly the George and Dragon) at Chesham has one wall painted with a stag-hunt over which a figure, presumably George I, presides. The other wall, which is damaged, is painted with flowers and birds in the manner of crewel embroidery. Although these two murals are in a small room (12 foot x 11 foot) their scale is large.

In America a number of writers, most notably Nina Fletcher Little, have studied the painted decoration to be found in the smaller American interiors of the first half-century following Independence, and particularly the use of stencils. The British tax on paper affected the sales of wallpaper in England (and America), and it was not until 1847 that the tax was lowered; in 1861 it was abolished. Before 1861 wallpaper was thus not much used in smaller English interiors.

In medieval Europe stencilling was widely used. The word itself is thought to derive from the Old French *estinceller*, to sparkle, to powder with stars. The process was common in England, although the Painter Stainers' Company of London discouraged the use of stencils as 'a false and deceiptful work and destructive to the art of painting, being a great hindrance of ingenuity and a cherisher of idleness and laziness in all beginners of the said

Stencilled wall decoration from 'Joscelyn's', Little Horkesley, near Colchester Essex.

art'.[4] Many examples survive from Jacobean times and before. The method was often used in conjunction with free-hand painting, or was simply used as a lining to a niche. The Victorian Gothic craftsmen reintroduced this technique, but evidence of its use in Britain in the intervening two centuries is scarce. Seventeenth and eighteenth-century wallpapers survive where stencilling has been used as an alternative to printing. Colchester Castle Museum contains fragments of four fine examples but a fifth late-eighteenth-century specimen is of particular interest. The stencilling is from a plaster wall with oak studs, the decoration being applied arbitrarily across the different surfaces and consisting of simple repeat patterns and a border which Nina Fletcher Little has remarked to the author closely resembles American stencilling. Francis Reader[6] found a number of examples in England in the 1930s and I have recently discovered some in and around Bath, all of which are painted (apparently in water-based colour) direct on to the surface, be it wood or plaster. Most examples are either

PLACE	DATE	DESIGN
1 Spencer's Belle Vue, Lansdown Road, Bath (in drawing room).	1788	Blue garlands.
The Crown Hotel, Aylesbury.	c. 1800	Old gold background with bunches of flowers and foliage stencilled in black, white and brown.
The Great House, Northleach, Glos. (Now demolished.)	c. 1800	Two designs found each in a different room, both of dots and leaves. (A third fragmentary example was found in this house.)
Lower Dairy Farm, Little Horkesley, Essex.	c. 1800	Painted on wood. Entwined ribbons and garlands in dark grey on white with a border of triangles and lozenges (apparently based on a design by Jean Pillement[8]).
5 Market Hill, Saffron Waldon, Essex.	c. 1800	Dots and foliage, dark green and sage with a border of flowers and triangles.
The Grove, Highgate, London. (Fragment now in the Victoria and Albert Museum.)	c. 1800	Stencilled in situ on eighteenth century wallpaper of which the design had been washed off.
18 New Bond Street, Bath (second floor back room).	c. 1812	Flowing design of foliage in darkish green.
22 Claverton Buildings, Claverton Street, Bath (ground floor back room).	c. 1815	Anthemion design in black on ivory.
4 Prior Park Cottages, Bath.	c. 1815	Fragments, design not known.
39 Grosvenor Place, Bath (third floor back room). These houses were designed by John Eveleigh but interiors were completed by John Pinch the Younger. This house, No. 39, also contains in the first floor front room a fine mural attributed to Thomas Shew, Architect and Painter.	begun in 1791, not finished until 1819 and not occupied until 1828	Floral design in black and terracotta on ivory.

1 Camden Terrace, Bath
(first floor front room).
Terrace designed by John
Pinch the Younger.

c. 1830–40 Rich floral design in
white on brown.

Cottage at Sharpstone,
Freshford, Nr. Bath.

c. 1840 Design in dark and light
blue on pink ground with
scroll. Painted on wood
matchboarding flanking
stairs, removed and
mostly destroyed in 1973.

Far left: *Original stencilled wall
decoration found at Lower Dairy
Farm, Little Horkesley with* (left) *a
modern reconstruction of the same
design. The entwined ribbons and
garlands are in dark grey on white.
c1800.*

Above: *Detail from stenciling on a
match-boarded wall in a cottage at
Sharpstone, Freshford, near Bath.
c1840.*

in small houses or in the lesser rooms of large ones. Possibly the earliest was found in the drawing-room of No. 1, Spencer's Belle Vue, Lansdown Road, Bath, built in 1788. 'It seemed to be in the form of stripes or garlands and the colour was blue.'[7] Unfortunately this type of work is usually discovered when walls are stripped before being re-papered. The decoration is then found to be in poor repair and is as a result covered up again rather than restored. Often the design goes unrecognised for what it is, householders assuming that it is simply the stain of an earlier wallpaper. Stencilling has certain characteristics which enable it to be recognised. Principal among these is the interruption of a line, the bridge which holds the stencil itself together. Most of the examples of interest that have been traced seem to date from the first years of the nineteenth century.

No doubt more examples will come to light. For the present I will have to turn to documentary evidence of the use of this technique in early nineteenth-century England. Loudon describes 'The Process of Stencilling Walls or Ceilings':

> The . . . mode of stenciling is the most common in Britain; by it, the patterns are all cut out in pastboard or oilcloth, and as many pieces of board or cloth are employed for each figure, or compartment, as there are colours or shades to be laid on. This mode of ornamenting the walls of rooms is not unsuitable for cottages of the humblest description, on account of its cheapness; and because, in remote places, or in new countries, it might be done by the cottager himself or by the local plasterer or house-painter.

Stencilled ceilings are known in America but I know of none in England. Neither have I found any English examples of stencilled floors or 'painted carpets' as they are known in America. Floors painted of one colour were, however, common in English cottages. Loudon stresses that the character of the stencilled designs employed should bear some relationship to the 'Architecture of the cottage' and that even:

> More judgement is required in the disposition than the choice of ornament . . . The side-walls of a room equally ornamented in every part by elaborate stencilng, or by rich paper, would be intolerable, were it not for the contrast produced by the plain ceiling, and by the border with which the paper, or stenciling is finished under the cornice at the top, and above the base or surbase below.

In the second half of the nineteenth century stencilling became very common for high quality work, and examples abound. Owen Jones in *The Grammar of Ornament* (1856)

illustrates 'Diapers'[9] that must have been used as the basis for many stencilled designs in Victorian church interiors. Stencil work was now proudly used for grand domestic interiors, as the *House Decorator and Painter's Guide* (1840) makes clear.[10] That which hitherto had been reserved for the poor was now too good for them. In *Healthy Homes and How to Make Them* (London 1854) William Bardwell put forward minimum building standards for his day. He recommends that paper should be hung on 'all the walls of the sitting and bed rooms of the dwellings with figured paper of the value of one penny per yard of approved designs . . .'

Ceilings in the humble houses of England were generally painted but undecorated. Earlier, in the seventeenth century, wind-dials were occasionally painted on ceilings in grand houses, and sundials were a type of practical decoration that was used in quite humble houses. 'A pretty way to make a Sun dyall on the seeling of a Room or Chamber, whereby you may know the time of day as you lie in Bed.'[11]

Scenic painting was commonly practised in America by folk artists of varying ability and Loudon describes such work as appropriate for *Cottage, Farm and Villa Architecture*:

> The perspective view . . . as an imitation of something existing, or supposed to exist, in nature, forms a whole with reference to itself, and not to the art by which it is produced, and consequently admits of almost endless variety.

Some years ago such a perspective view was discovered under four layers of wallpaper in a house in Bath, No. 39 Grosvenor Place. It has been attributed to Thomas Shew. Captain H. Marsh was the first occupier of the house in 1828 and the mural presumably dates from this period.[12] Thomas Shew lived at this time two doors away from Captain Marsh. Other wall paintings are known in Bath at No. 2 Lansdown Terrace and at No. 1 The Circus. Their quality is varied but in spirit they attempt to be nothing but decorative.

Related to the scenic wall paintings were the similarly painted 'transparent blinds' so fully described in Nathaniel Whittock's *The Decorative Painters' and Glaziers' Guide* (London 1827). Plate XLIV in Whittock's book illustrates in colour a fine example of such a blind painted with a classical landscape; another illustration, in black and white, demonstrates a 'blind properly strained' on a framework reminiscent of a quilting frame and shows a fine view of a romantic gothic castle. Whittock makes the point about stencilling transparent blinds (Chapter V, p. 188) that those who have 'succeeded in painting landscapes in distemper on walls, or in water colour on paper, will find he has acquired the power of painting transparent blinds'. These

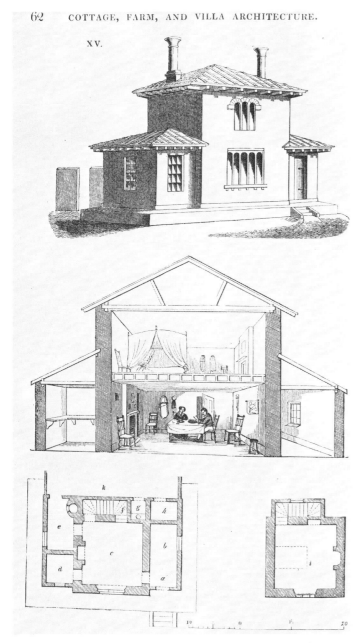

XV.

'Cottage dwellings' as seen by J. C. Loudon in An Encyclopædia of Cottage, Farm and Village Architecture *(1857).*

blinds were made of 'Scotch cambric or lawn which can be procured in almost any width for this purpose'. Smaller blinds were painted with pigments held with isinglass dissolved by boiling 'but for large blinds of the dimensions of a common sash window parchment size' was used. Blinds of this type appear in an engraving of a view of an Ameri-

can interior showing a quilting party that appeared in *Gleason's Pictorial* in October 21, 1854—clearly such blinds were equally popular in the United States. This engraving, though with slightly different window blinds was later copied by an unknown American folk artist.

Floors

In the seventeenth century and before, imported oriental carpets were not put to the indignity of being placed upon the floor; they were used as table carpets. As 'Turkey' carpets became more common they descended to the floor. Rushes and rush matting were the common sort of floor covering. Loudon states that 'Matting is manufactured in many different manners, out of straw of corn, rushes or other long, narrow, grassy or sedgy leaves . . . Matting of this sort might in some cases be employed as partitions, and is extensively used in the more miserable of the cottages both in France and Scotland'. Some quite fine houses of the eighteenth century seem to have been content with bare floorboards, as shown in pictures by Arthur Devis and others.

By the nineteenth century mass-produced Scotch and Kidderminster carpets were, on account of their cheapness, 'the kinds of carpets most suitable for cottages'. Even so, 'for neither the parlour nor the bed-room would we recommend the carpet to be fitted to the room'. Instead Loudon suggests

> A square of carpet [which] may be changed eight times so as to be worn equally in every part of both sides. For a cottage's bed-room, we would chiefly recommend one piece of carpeting placed by the dressing-table, and pieces neatly fitted to each other to go round the foot and sides of the bed. Stair carpets give an air of great comfort and finish to a house; and a cottage should never be without one.

The painted carpets of New England are not found in Britain. Perhaps because of our early industrialisation this answer to floor covering does not seem to have been adopted here, neither do we seem to have painted floors to simulate marble. However, Loudon does describe the type of treatment that a floor should be given

> When a parlour carpet does not cover the whole of the floor . . . Some recommend oil-cloth, others baize, drugget, coarse broadcloth, or brown linen; for our part, we greatly prefer to any of these, painting that part

of the boards of the floor which is not covered with the carpet, of the same colour as the woodwork of the room . . . This is by far the best mode in staircases and in bed-rooms, as well as in parlours; it also saves a great deal of the most disagreeable part of a woman's household labours.

After some discussion of colour schemes for carpets, walls and curtains ('A yellow carpet may have black curtains, and a dark grey paper with yellow borders and ornaments'), Loudon looks briefly at 'Geographical Carpets'. He concludes this section by adding that 'A map such as above described, might, however, be printed on fine cloth, on brown holland linen, and might serve as a cover to a carpet. This would be particularly suitable for a school-room or nursery.' In alluding to 'The idea of a geographical carpet . . .' he seems to be describing a memory of the Ditchley portrait of Queen Elizabeth I.

The 1763 trade label for the turner, Alexander Wetherstone, shows his sign to have been 'ye Painted Floor Cloth and Brush'.[13] This is one of the earliest references that I have been able to find to such floor covering being used in Britain, although its widespread use in America has long been established. John Smith (*The Art of Painting*, 1676) mentions oil-cloth, not for use on floors but rather as being suitable waterproofing for clothes. 'An Experiment relating to Oyl Colours of great use to Travellers of Some kinds: To the chief Officers of Camps and Armies, to Seamen and such like.' The Wetherstone floor cloth is a simple geometric design of alternating black and white lozenges with a compass rose in the centre. It appears to imitate the marble floors, designs for which appeared in Batty Langley's 1750 *The Builder's and Workman's Treasury of Designs;* for example, 'Irregular Octogons and Geometrical Squares' and 'Parallelopipedons and Cubes Erect.'

Inevitably Loudon has a section on painted floor cloths:

> *Painted Floorcloths* may sometimes be used in lobbies and passages of cottages; but they are not economical articles, where there is much going out and coming in of persons generally employed in the open air, and of course wearing strong shoes, probably with nails in the soles. When they are used in cottages, the most appropriate patterns are imitations or some materials usually employed for floors, such as tressellated pavement, different-coloured stones, etc; but, for the better description of dwellings, where oilcloths are considered chiefly as ornamental coverings, there seems to be no reason why their patterns should not be as various as those of carpets.

The deck of Queen Victoria's royal yacht was covered with oil cloth painted to simulate planking[14] and in the officer's

Above: *Sign for Alexander Wetherstone at 'Ye Painted Floor Cloth and Brush in Portugal Street, near Lincoln's Inn back gate. 1763'.*

quarters, the decks of Nelson's *H.M.S. Victory* were covered with canvas, painted with a pattern of black and white squares[15].

Loudon also describes 'Paper Carpets' as being made by 'cutting out and sewing together pieces of linen, cotton, Scotch-gauze, canvas, or any similar materal', sizing it as necessary 'and carefully pasting it round the margins so as to keep it tight . . . When the cloth thus fixed is dry, lay on it two or more coats of strong paper, breaking joint, and finish with coloured or hanging paper according to fancy'. These appear to have been a type of home-made linoleum. Clearly a great deal of work was put into making various floor coverings but unfortunately few if any early oil cloths or paper carpets survive. A particular loss is a type of patchwork carpet described by Loudon as follows:

> Remnants of cloth bought from the woollen-draper, or taylor, and cut into any kind of geometrical shapes, may be sewed together, so as to form circles, stars, or any other regular figures that may be desired; and, when arranged with taste, produce a very handsome and desirable carpet at a trifling expense . . .

Furniture

While provincial furniture is often to be met with in Britain, peasant or folk work is much less common. As Eric Mercer

Right: *Mid–19th century transparent blind made from cotton lawn painted with the aid of stencils. 96in x 60in.*

has remarked in *Furniture 700–1700*[16] 'Early timber furniture has survived less well, but its direct successors in eighteenth and nineteenth century Scandinavian peasant houses probably reflect its qualities . . .' This tendency for the high style of yesterday to become the folk style of today is characteristic of folk culture in general. That is why

> In one way, of course, the painting of furniture has never ceased and much of the painted peasant furniture still common enough in Austria and Scandinavia and parts of Germany, is of the eighteenth and nineteenth centuries. The important difference however is that in early years even the best furniture of kings was often painted, while later painting was usually confined to the furniture of lesser men or to the less important furniture of the great.[17]

In general there is very little furniture in Britain made specifically for the sub-culture that goes above and beyond the needs of utility. Although post-medieval cottage furniture was often carved and sometimes painted, it was almost never embellished with painted decoration. The interiors of sailors' chests and canal-boat cabins are among the exceptions, though furniture of the nineteenth century was often grained. Most cottage furniture in Britain was in a style which was either a remote survival of Elizabethan or Jacobean forms, such as the court cupboard and dresser, or a pale and provincial version of metropolitan taste.

Left: A group of English country furniture: a three-legged table with a fine burr oak top; a Windsor chair in ash and beech – the paintwork is contemporary; a four-legged stool in elm and ash.

Below and right: *Straw cradle and 'Beehive' easy chair.*

In very remote places like the Shetland Islands, true and independent furniture forms were able to develop unmolested by the mainland. But these islands have, if anything, more kinship with Scandinavia than with Scotland. The Shetland Island chair constructed of wood and rushes has become well known. Similar chairs must have once been quite common in the British Isles. Loudon says that 'In Monmouthshire, easy chairs with hoods, like porters chairs in gentlemens halls, are constructed of straw matting on a frame of wooden rods, or of stout iron wire; and [some] chairs . . . are made entirely of straw in different parts of England, in the same way as the common beehives'.[18]

Though furniture is a significant and recognisable part of the folk art of most other countries, it has little if any

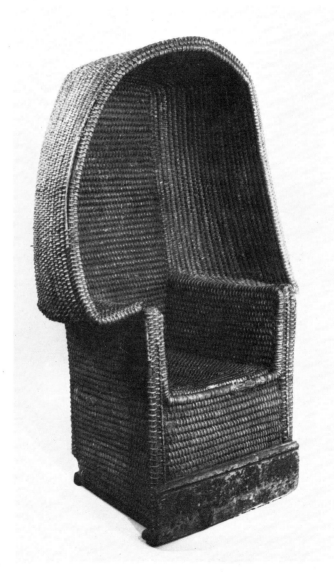

Above: *A country-made Windsor style chair.*
Right: *An early 18th century Windsor settee in elm.*

significance in Britain. In America, for example, painted furniture almost invariably owes its inspiration to non-British immigrants, most notably the Germans. The American windsor chair differs from its British cousin in many respects, but one of the points that they have in common is that both were traditionally painted, dark green and dark red being popular colours. In Britain ignorance of this tradition has meant that many of these garden chairs have lost their original paint. Yew wood chairs intended for use inside the home were left uncoloured, leaving the beauty of this wood to speak for itself.

3   J. T. Smith, *Nollekens and his Times*, 1919 ed., vol. II, page 102. Capitsoldi had been a student of the Roman sculptor Algardi. He subsequently returned to Italy.
4   W. A. D. Englefield, *History of the Painter Stainers' Company*, pages 95–6.
5   Nina Fletcher Little, in a letter to the author, 10 May 1974.
6   *Archaeological Journal*, vol. XCV, 1938, 'Mural Decoration' by Francis W. Reader.
7   Mrs I. E. Bonfield, the owner of the house, in a letter to the author, 8 February 1974.
8   Robert Sayer, *The Ladies Amusement or Whole Art of Japaning Made Easy*, London, c.1760, plate 118, 'Borders'.
9   Owen Jones, *The Grammar of Ornament*, 1856, chapter 16, 'Medieval Ornament', plate 68.
10   H. W. and A. Arrowsmith, *The House Decorator and Painter's Guide*, London, 1840.
11   John White, *A Rich Cabinet with a Variety of Inventions*, London, 1651.
12   *Bath Chronicle*, 20 July 1955.
13   In the Ambrose Heal Collection, Department of Prints and Drawings, British Museum.
14   Virginia Surtees, *Charlotte Canning*, London, 1975.
15   Carola Oman, *Nelson*, paperback ed. Sphere Books, London, page 462.
16   Eric Mercer, *Furniture 700–1700*, London, 1969, page 30.
17   Ibid., page 43.
18   J. C. Loudon, *An Encyclopaedia of Cottage, Farm and Villa Architecture and Furniture* (first published in London, 1836), page 347.

1   See Margaret Jourdain, *English Interior Decoration 1500–1830*.
2   John Stalker and George Parker, *A Treatise of Japaning*, Oxford, 1688, chapter 26.

Domestic Crafts

The higher crafts are dependent upon a living tradition. They cannot be learnt from a book; they can be taught only by example. Wood-carving at the higher levels is such a craft, whereas I should venture to suggest that knitting can be learnt from a pattern-book. The one demands years of apprenticeship and innate ability, whereas the other only requires application. Traditionally, working in wood has been a masculine occupation. Textiles, however, have not always been exclusive to the distaff side. Apart from the sailors' woolwork pictures, knitting was another activity indulged in by men. Howitt, writing of the Dales of Yorkshire in his book *Rural Life of England* published in 1840, records the following information:

> Knitting is a great practice in the dales. Men, women, and children, all knit. Formerly you might have met the wagoners knitting as they went along with their teams; but this is now rare; for the greater influx of visitors, and their wonder expressed at this and other practices has made them rather ashamed of some of them, and shy of strangers observing them. But the men still knit a great deal in the houses; and the women knit incessantly.*

Necessity was the mother of invention for most cottage crafts, but the working day lasted as long as the hours of daylight and, during the harvest moon, longer. Artificial light was extremely limited and many of these crafts were performed in almost total darkness. Again I must refer to Howitt:

> As soon as it becomes dark, and the usual business of the day is over . . . they rake or put out the fire; take their cloaks and lanterns and set out with their knitting to the house of the neighbour where the sitting falls in rotation, for it is a regularly circulating assembly from house to house . . . The whole troop of neighbours being collected, they sit and knit, sing knitting songs, and tell knitting-stories. . . . All this time their

knitting goes on with unremitting speed. They sit rocking to and fro like so many weird wizards. They burn no candle, but knit by the light of the peat fire . . .*

The provision of artificial light was expensive, but for some crafts firelight was insufficient. Candles were extremely expensive. Until the end of the eighteenth century wax candles cost thirty shillngs a pound and even with the development of whaling, spermaceti candles were also expensive: 'April 14 1758 . . . 1 dozen spermaceti candles no. 3, to the pound, £1.7.0'[1] This sort of expenditure was beyond the means of cottagers. In the nineteenth century oil-lamps were widely used in America but they were not so common in Britain. Rushlight was meagre but it was the best that cottagers could afford. The rushes were collected in late summer or autumn:

> You peels away the rind from the peth, leavin' only a little strip of rind, and when the rushes is dry you dips 'em in grease, keepin' 'em well under; and my mother she always laid hers to dry in a bit of hollow bark. Mutton fat's the best, it dries hardest.[2]

Gilbert White in his *Natural History of Selborne* states that a good rush, two feet four inches long, would burn for 57 minutes and that rushes costing three shillings per lb. went 1,600 to the lb. In the nineteenth century a candle would occasionally be used even in a cottage, if more light were essential. Sometimes even this extravagance provided insufficient light, in which case the candle-light would be magnified with a water-filled clear glass globe. In England such a globe was known as a 'flash'.[3] The earliest reference that I have found to this device appears in John White's *A Rich Cabinet with a Variety of Inventions* (1651):

> *How to make a glorious light with a Candle like the Sun-shine.* This is a rare Conceit fit for those Artists or others that perform curious and fine works by Candle-light as Jewellers, Ingravers, or the like, or

---

*Page 237. 'The old men' sat so close to the fire 'that they pin cloths on their shins to prevent their being burnt'.

*Howitt explains that these meetings were known as a Sitting or 'Going-a-sitting'.

115

shal have a glorious light through the Glaffe, and water for your purpofe; behold the Figure following.

Some ufe to place a fheet of oyled paper betwixt them & a candle, and this will caufe a good light.

those which are weake sighted to read by, never dazeling the Eye.

Goe to the Glass House, or Glass-shop, and let them blow you a thin Globe glass, bigger than a penny Loaf (the bigger the better) with a short neck like a Bottle, they know how to make them. When you have this Glasse, with Glew or Wax bind a piece of Tape or Pack-thread about the neck or top, making a little loop therewith to hang by; Then fill your Glasse with the purest Conduit or Spring-water you can get (putting some Aqua-vitae therin to keep it from freezing) stopping it close to keep the dust out, having thus done, if you will use it at a Table or Bench, knock a Tenter-hooke or Naile into the Seeling or Shelf and with a Tape or Pack-thread fasten it to the loope and hang it up (but a round stick were better to hang it on, putting it in-to a poast or hole in the wall, that you may let it higher or lower at your pleasure in turning the stick). Then behind your Glass set a Candle lighted upon a Table, and you shal have a glorious light through the Glasse . . .

Light was one of the practical considerations that limited and disciplined the crafts of the cottagers.

Treen

Small objects, utilitarian or otherwise, made of wood are known as 'treen'. All interested in this subject are indebted to Edward H. Pinto's collection (now at Birmingham City Museum and Art Gallery) and his book, *Treen and Other Wooden Bygones*, (Bell, London 1969).

Although wood is an extremely difficult material to carve, the amateur was quite capable of 'chip carving', which is fundamentally two-dimensional. Form was more difficult, but simple shapes were possible. Many of these objects were labours of love and as such were given to sweethearts. The Welsh love spoon is perhaps the most famous example. These spoons are, more often than not, made of sycamore, although other close-grained woods with a close texture were used, such as yew, a 'softwood' which is much harder than many 'hardwoods'.* Many wooden spoons were of course made for use, such as the Caernarvon crooked spoons which were possibly made for children or invalids, and those made for eating porridge or the bacon and leek broth

Top: *From John White's* A Rich Cabinet with Variety of Inventions *(1651)*.
Above: *A lacemaker working with the aid of just such a light as that described by White.*

*Deciduous trees are known as 'hardwoods', for example balsa wood (which is very soft), in contrast to the evergreen yew, a 'softwood' (which is hard).

116

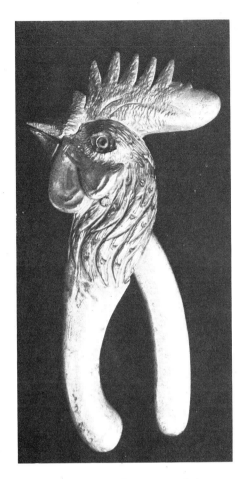

A pair of nutcrackers carved from wood in the form of a cockerel; a knitting stick or sheath in carved wood; a group of Welsh love spoons.

known as 'cawl'. Most early love spoons, in fact, were usable; the later ones were often simply seen as Diana's 'trophies of the chase'. The earliest dated specimen in the collection of the National Museum of Wales is from the years 1667.

Once these spoons had been freed from the requirements of necessity they became extravagant, extraordinary and sometimes grotesque in shape. They were decorated with many emblems of love and devotion. The number of bowls, it is thought, refer to the number of hoped-for children, with one large bowl to symbolise the lovers as two in one, reinforced with a sprinkling of hearts and keyholes. The comma shape that is also used on these spoons was emblematic of the soul and is thought to derive from Ancient Egypt. An example containing all of these elements in the Pinto Collection measures twenty-nine inches by five and a quarter inches, and as well as these ancient symbols it

incorporates a hobby-horse cycle and a representation of Telford's Menai suspension bridge, which dates the spoon to *c.* 1820–30.

The majority of these later Welsh love spoons, as useless objects, were utterly romantic. This was not always the case elsewhere, for many a lover seems to have directed his sweetheart back to the household chores. The Pinto Collection, among its many treasures, includes a unique yew-wood basting stick and a large collection of knitting sticks or cases, most of which seem to have been made as professions of love. Knitting sticks or sheaths average between eight and nine inches in length but can be as small as three inches or as long as a foot. Some of these were made in North Wales, but many must have been made in the Yorkshire and Westmorland Dales where knitting was such an important feature of life and where a particular knitting technique evolved: *

> . . . this rocking motion [of the body] is connected
> with a mode of knitting peculiar to the place, called

*Knitting sticks with nautical symbols were no doubt made by sailors.

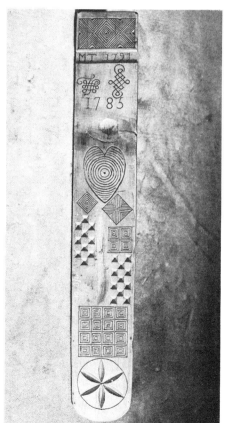

Above: *A fisherwoman knitting in Cornwall.*
Right: *A stay busk inscribed with the names of Thomas and Elizabeth Underwood, c1780.*
Far right, top: *A knitting stick with hooks to catch up the work.*
Far right, bottom: *A carved stay busk inscribed with initials and two dates.*

swaving, which is difficult to describe. Ordinary knitting is performed by a variety of little motions, but this is a single uniform tossing motion of both the hands at once, and the body often accompanying it with a sort of sympathetic action. The knitting produced is just the same as by the ordinary method. They knit with crooked pins called pricks; and use a knitting-sheath consisting commonly of a hollow piece of wood, as large as the sheath of a dagger, curved to the side, and fixed in a belt called the cowband. The women of the north, in fact, often sport very curious knitting sheaths. We have seen a wisp of straw tied up pretty tightly, into which they stick their needles; and sometimes a bunch of quills of at least half-a-hundred in number. These sheaths and cowbands are often presents from their lovers to the young women. Upon the band there is a hook, upon which the long end of the knitting is suspended that it may not dangle. In this manner they knit for the Kendal market, stockings, jackets, nightcaps, and a kind of cap worn by the negroes, called bump-caps. These are made of very coarse worsted, and knit a yard in length, one half of which is turned into the other, before it has the appearance of a cap.[1]*

Knitting was practised in the north of England by people of many social orders:

In such a place [as Wensleydale]† a man's appearance is no indication of his actual condition as respects property . . . They tell a story with great glee, of an old Friend, John Wilkinson, who sat in a patched coat on a large stone by the road-side, knitting, when a gentleman riding by stopped and fixed his eyes on him as in compassion, and then threw him half-a-crown. He picked it up, told him he was much obliged to him, and added—'May be I'se richer na tou', and returned him the money . . . In fact the old Friend was wealthy . . .

Lone knitting was not very popular. More often it was a group activity stimulated by knitting-songs. Celia Fiennes when touring East Anglia in 1698 recorded in her diary, 'the ordinary people knitting four or five in a company under the hedges.'

Being such an intimate part of the structure of the traditional female costume the busk or stay was a natural subject for the love token. These were usually slightly longer than knitting sticks, allowing more room for decoration and the addition of a dedicatory verse. The earliest known example is dated 1660, also the period of the earliest dated love spoon.

While the folk art of food would clearly reward research this is not the concern of the present book. However, the subject of treen would not be complete without some passing reference to carved wood gingerbread and butter moulds, many of which could be purchased at the fair:

At all the stalls, purchases of gingerbread, sweet-meats, nuts and oranges are going on . . . Tea-caddies, work-boxes of rosewood and pearl, china, cut glass, clowns and trumpets, and all kinds of toys; bracelets and necklaces, and all species of female trinkets; fans, and parlour bellows, figures in porcelain and painted wood; purses, musical boxes, and in short, all the thousand contents of a bazaar.[4]

*Knitters received three pence for each such cap.
†In this valley people live 'like ancient kings in the rude abundance of earthly plenty' where some maintain 'the primitive custom of two meals a day from Candlemas to Martinmas, which is the depth of winter. They breakfast at ten o'clock on cold meat, ale, cheese, etc; and do not go into the house again till six in the evening.'

A carved wooden gingerbread mould with the initials DHC on the bottom.

Carved relief obeys a convention that is difficult to obey. To carve these moulds, so to say, 'inside out and backwards' is the more remarkable. For this reason gingerbread, sugar and butter moulds were the work of professionals.

119

Toys

High Victorian toys, especially those made of wood, were left remarkably uncorrupted by the prevailing standards set set by theoretical designers. A painting of the Lowther Arcade by an unknown Victorian includes in the composition a couple of shops displaying charmingly naïve wooden toys destined for the nurseries of the upper classes, though *Dickens's Dictionary of London* describes the arcade as 'a bazaar principally for cheap toys and mosaic jewellery'. Lowther Arcade was described in *Gaslight and Daylight* by George Augustus Sala:

I have no room for statistics, so I will not enter into any calculation as to the numerical quantities of fancy wares vended in Lowther Arcade; . . . I may passingly observe, that there are toys, and gems, and knick-knacks here, that are things of great price today, and positive drugs in the market tomorrow. At one time the public toy-taste runs upon monkeys that run up sticks, or old gentlemen that swing by their own door-knockers, squeaking dreadfully the while; at another period the rage is for the squeezeable comic masks and faces (at first fallaciously supposed to be made of gutta-percha, but ultimately discovered, through the agency of a precocious philosopher, aged seven—who ate one of them—to be formed from a composition of glue, flour and treacle). Now, horrible writhing gutta-percha snakes are up, and now they are down; now pop-guns go off and now hang fire.

Left: *The Lowther Arcade painted by an unknown artist; now in the possession of Coutts Bank.*
Above: *An early 19th century rocking horse.*

There are certain toys and fancy ornaments that always, however, preserve a healthy vogue, and command a ready sale. Of the former, the Noah's arks, and dolls' houses, and India rubber balls, may be mentioned, although their nominal nomenclatures are sometimes altered to suit the exigencies of fashion. Thus we are enticed to purchase Uncle Buncle's Noah's Ark, Peter Parley's rubber balls, or Jenny Lind's Doll's mansion . . .

Most popular was the rocking horse whose cousins on the roundabouts were no less sought after for rides by an even wider social range. The hobby horse, (later developed into a tricycle horse) has an even older history and may be regarded as their common ancestor. Such things were made by professional craftsmen, as was the Noah's Ark and its inhabitants—German immigrants to Britain. The Noah's Ark owed much of its popularity to the fact that because of its religious significance it was one of the few toys allowed out on Sundays.

Some toys were educational in inspiration. One example is the Nürnberg kitchen, used to teach little girls in Germany one of the three Ks. In Britain model butcher's shops seem to have fulfilled the same function; they were certainly not designed to be 'played' with as most were displayed behind glass in a cross-banded mahogany shadow-box.* I have seen a total of about ten butcher's shops of this type but I know of only three three-dimensional

*Pedlar dolls displayed under glass shades were similarly designed to be looked at and not played with.

Above: *Two late 19th century models of butcher's shops with a variety of goods on display.*

examples that are accessible as playthings: one in the Bethnal Green Museum, one in the Judkyn Collection and

made 'pub' toys such as the race-horse game. These horses of carved wood were made as a series. They would be placed upon an inn table and, with their counter-balances set in motion, the one that 'ran' the longest was declared the winner. Some of these counter-balance equestrian groups include rather smart military figures and were perhaps designed as toys rather than as gambling devices. The following collections each have an example: The Castle Museum, York; The Judkyn Collection, Bath, and the Museum of the Society for the Preservation of New England Antiquities, Boston.

In fact the number of toys and dolls made by both the amateur and the professional with artistic flair, for both children and adults, is without number. Most that may be classed as folk art were of wood, but in the case of wooden dolls the clothes were of equal, if not greater, importance. Judging by nineteenth-century portraits of children, pull-along toys were popular. A superb example is illustrated as the frontispiece of Patrick Murray's *Toys* (Studio Vista/Dutton, 1968). It represents a Kentish hop-cart drawn by four horses, dating from about 1820.

In general toys were professionally made and sold to the middle and upper classes. It is unlikely that children of the working class had much opportunity for play and even their more fortunate contemporaries were expected to work at their studies rather than 'waste time' with toys and games.

Scale models or miniatures are in a different class and involve a mental outlook that is systematic rather than inventive, measured rather than instinctive and therefore not conducive to the sort of artistry with which we are concerned.

Textiles

Traditionally both animal and vegetable sources have been used to provide the thread from which many types of cloth have been woven. Mineral sources of cloth were once the most exclusive, cloth-of-gold being but one example. Today synthetic fibres of chemical origin are the cheapest. In northern Europe the most common animal fibre to be transformed into cloth was wool, and the most common vegetable, linen.

If the view that folk art is a post-medieval phenomenon is accepted, then the early emergence of industrialisation in Britain, coupled with a traditional preoccupation with the cloth trade, conspired to increase the industrialisation of that activity above all others. The Luddites could not stem

Top: *A doll's house in the form of a High Victorian villa, made by Thomas Risley and dated 1889.*
Above: *A toy stage coach, c1830.*

the third in the Museum of Childhood, Edinburgh. Baby houses, as they were known before the mid-nineteenth century, or dolls' houses as they were later called, were too expensive for 'ordinary' children. Many of the finest were designed to enchant adults and were strictly for contemplation; even the less elaborate examples were generally for rather grand nurseries. 'Baby' stable blocks are also known.

Many toys, for both children and adults, were doubtless made by amateurs. The man who made love spoons surely made dolls for the children he begat. No doubt he also the inevitability of this development and, as a consequence of it, the amount of homespun produced in the cottages of England was not very substantial in the nineteenth century, and few earlier examples survive. Most of this activity was confined to Scotland, Wales and Ireland, and the more remote parts of England.

Knitting Some attention has been given to knitting and knitting sticks in Yorkshire earlier in this chapter. For this work knitting-songs were used to develop a rhythm for work that helped to maintain speed:

> Bell-wether o'Barking,* cries baa baa,
> How many sheep have we lost to day?
> Nineteen have we lost, one have we fun,
> Run Rockie,† run Rockie, run, run, run.

The next verse was used to accompany the next round of a stocking:

> Bell-wether o'Barking, cries baa, baa,
> How many sheep have we lost to day?
> Eighteen have we lost, two have we fun,
> Run Rockie, run Rockie, run, run, run.

*A mountain overlooking Dent Dale.
†A sheep-dog.

It was thus that peasants in the north of England used the 'count down', compensated by the 'count up', to accelerate their work. These songs alluded to their way of life or occupation but the knitting that they produced was in general of the simplest utilitarian kind, although decorative knitting is found on the Yorkshire coast where fishermen's jerseys or guernseys were made. The designs tend to be associated with particular villages and it has sometimes been thought that this was to help with the identification of the bodies of those who perished at sea. The Scottish and Irish islands are renowned for distinctive patterns, many of which form part of the repertoire of a living craft.

Smocking The English peasant does not have a very distinct cultural identity as compared with other countries,

Left: *Girl knitting a sweater on Inisheer in the Aran Islands, County Galway.*
Below: *A smock worn in Norfolk in 1902.*

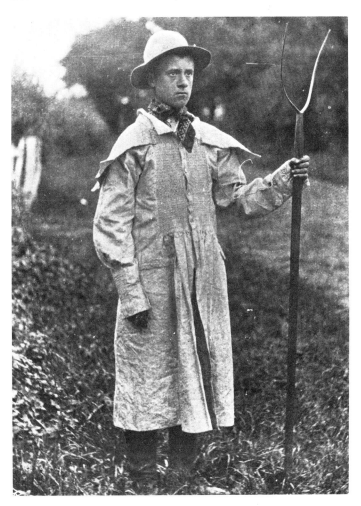

and Industrialisation may to some extent account for this. As a result the British Isles have a remarkable poverty of traditional dress. In Ireland 'the ascendency' carried out the British policy of suppressing anything that might inspire nationalism such as language or dress. In Scotland the plaid has an ancient history but the tartans and kilts in their present form are thought by some to have been the creation of Sir Walter Scott at the instigation of Queen Victoria. In Wales nineteenth-century romanticism resulted in the revival of the high-crowned hat of the seventeenth century in a new conical form worn by women. It could be argued that England lost her peasant culture because of industrialisation and before nineteenth-century romanticism had a chance of encouraging and preserving it. On the other hand it could be said, somewhat perversely, that there was in England an exception, an exception that gives England an almost greater claim to a national dress than other parts of Britain. I refer to the smock.

The earliest examples extant date from the late eighteenth century. They fall into two categories: the *round frock* and the *coat frock*. The tailoring of these garments, particularly the round frock, was extremely simple and the *smocking* grew out of the need to 'absorb' excess material around the torso and shoulders at the same time as providing an extra thickness of material as weather-proofing. Howitt in his *Rural Life of England* suggests that the different designs indicated the various occupations of their wearers, but there is no evidence to support this. Newark-on-Trent was an important source for smocks in the Midlands, where they were known as 'Newark Frocks'. There were four main types of smock within the two categories found in four main regions. The very simple smock of Sussex and Surrey, which has only slight gathers and little embroidery, contrasts with the large panels of smocking and big embroidered collars found in the western counties of England and in Wales. In Hampshire, Somerset, Gloucestershire and the Midlands, simple smocks were elaborately decorated. In East Anglia a boat-necked smock with a roll collar seems to have been preferred.

Smocks were made of a tough twill known as 'drabbet' and are commonly thought to have been left a natural, off-white colour. However, this was not the case and to some extent the colour that smocks were dyed helps to identify the regions in which they were made:

> In the counties round London, eastward and westward through Berkshire, Hampshire, Wiltshire, etc. the

A smock from Sussex; a mid–19th century Somerset smock made from twill, known as 'drabbet'; a smock from Buckinghamshire made c1870.

124

English peasant, shepherd and drover is the white-smocked man of the London prints. In Herefordshire and in that direction, he sports an olive-green smock. In the Midland counties, specially Leicestershire, Derby, Nottingham, Warwick and Staffordshire, he dons a blue smock called the 'Newark frock', which is finely gathered, in a square piece of parchment on the back and breast, on the shoulders and wrists; is adorned also in those parts with flourishes of white thread, and as invariably has a little white heart stitched in at the bottom of the slit in the neck.[4]

Some smocks were home made, and these tend to be the more elaborate wedding smocks passed down from one

Smock from Radnor.
Bottom: *A Pearly King and Queen with their children.*

generation to the next. The Victoria and Albert Museum owns an example of such a smock said to have been made for a wedding at Mayfield parish church in 1779. In every county the best or Sunday smock was white linen with white embroidery, and inevitably it is these 'Sunday best' smocks that have been preserved.

In the nineteenth century the Cockney devised his own 'national dress'. The Pearly costumes for men, women and children were a true folk expression not imposed from above. Unlike the basic smock designed as a working garment, these black velvet suits burdened with a considerable weight of pearl buttons were worn on high days, holidays and bonfire nights. Henry Croft a roadsweeper and rat catcher of Somerstown who died in 1930 at the age of 68 is credited with introducing the pearly suit. He wore the first such suit in about 1880 as the first Pearly King.[5]

Patchwork and Quilting Although the techniques involved are similar to those employed by the heraldic banner and flag makers of the middle ages, existing examples of patchwork in Britain go back only a couple of centuries. Most surviving specimens date from the nineteenth century or later and are made of cotton. Other materials such as wool and silk had always been used to some extent but these became most common after about 1870 when the Victorian 'throw' was fashionable. Patchwork was in origin a means of piecing together a series of otherwise unusable scraps, but it was soon developed into a controlled art form using textiles purchased for the purpose. Pieced or mosaic patchwork was a method that usually employed geometric shapes tacked over templates and sewn edge to edge with neighbouring pieces. As a tour-de-force, non-geometric forms were sometimes used—it is extremely difficult to handle material on the bias. Out of the basic elements of squares, diamonds, pentagons, hexagons, octagons, shells and stripes, used exclusively or in concert, many designs could be produced. Their strongly geometric character is so dominant and timeless that such patchwork is difficult to date. Only the materials provide a clue.

Textiles were printed in England with woodblocks until 1752 when Francis Nixon (1705–65) of the Drumcondra Printworks introduced engraved copper plates for this purpose.[6] By the early nineteenth century engraved copper roller-printed cottons were abundant and relatively cheap, but decorative textiles encouraged the production of patchwork at this time. Special centre-piece designs were manufactured for appliqué patchwork, a technique that is more suitable for free forms. Applied work in silk and velvet was fashionable for church furnishings and vestments until the fall in the price of silk resulted in its decline in the early

125

Above left: *An unusual patchwork quilt illustrating the story of Adam and Eve in the Garden of Eden with other scenes including Noah's Ark, Cain and Abel and the Conway Bridge. Mid–19th century.*

Left: *Centre of a patchwork quilt, c1805. This panel shows Napoleon's retreat from Moscow. The border of the quilt is made up from smaller panels of patriotic figures, military engagements and life at home.*

Above: *This pieced mosaic patchwork, c1800, is unfinished and still has some of the paper templates in place.*

eighteenth century. Appliqué work, though, continued as a folk craft. Sometimes a coverlet will be found that has a central square in appliqué 'framed' by pieced patches. Surviving examples suggest regional variations. In Ireland, the north of England and in Wales geometric designs predominate. Elizabeth Hake in her *English Quilting, Old and New* mentions an old lady she knew in Devon who told her of her mother's and grandmother's recollections of going out into the countryside picking sprays of oak leaves, ivy, clover and thistles on which to base patchwork designs.

Patchwork was often, but by no means always quilted.

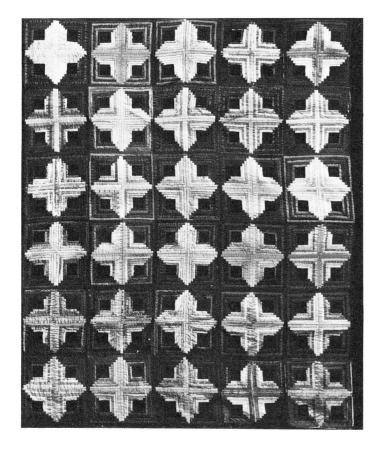

Above: *A Welsh quilt worked in the geometric design known as 'Log Cabin'.*
Above right: *A fine quilt with a feather motif from Henllan Ameoed, Carmarthenshire.*
Right: *A 19th century appliqué floral patchwork quilt.*

In poor households, especially in South Wales, patchwork linings were used only for reasons of economy beneath plain quilted tops. These linings were composed of patches of irregular size not designed to be seen. In those regions where quilting was considered a superior craft to patchwork as in the county of Durham, plain materials were employed to show to best advantage the work of professional quilters. These people drew out the entire design in a blue pencil. The amateurs moved over the cloth section by section with templates as the cloth was rolled out on the quilting frame. As is so often the case with the decorative arts quilting was functional in origin. It was simply a means of holding, by stitching, the top of a quilt to its lining with a 'fill' of wool or cotton. This practical need was used to decorative effect in Ancient China, pre-Columbian Mexico and medieval Europe.

Men are known to have made designs for these works as for other forms of needlework. Many haberdashers in the past, as today, also sold patterns. The trade card of Francis Bishop at the 'Sign of the Sun and Dove in King's Street, Bloomsbury Square' describes him as a 'haberdasher, glover, pattern drawer'; another haberdasher, Francis Flower at the 'Sign of the Rose and Woolsack' undertook to draw 'all sorts of Patterns' and sold 'shades of silk and canvas for working . . . all sorts of threads . . .'[8] Walter Gale of Sussex was another of these professional designers. He recorded in his diary for 26 December 1750 the following information:

> I began to draw the quilt belonging to Mrs Godman Dec 30th. I finished the bed quilt after five days close application. It gave great satisfaction and I received 10s 6d for the drawing.[9]

Little is known of the background of these designers. The Northumbrian Joseph Hedley is an exception and were it not for the fact that he died dramatically, the victim of murder, in January 1825, little would be known of his life. He was apprenticed as a tailor and it is likely that his interest in quilting began with work on cord-quilted waistcoats. His reputation for this work was such that he became known as Joe the Quilter. A white cotton quilt in the Bowes Museum is attributed to him.

A feather motif was a favourite device of George Gardiner. He was the village shopkeeper at Allenheads, Northumberland, in the nineteenth century and he taught many north-country women the art of quiltmaking, among them Miss Elizabeth Sanderson (d. 1934). It should not be supposed that all the great quilt designers were men. Mary Jones (d. 1900) of the village of Panteg, Cardiganshire, was a fine quilter who took many pupils. In South Wales the itinerant quilters did much to maintain and spread their tradition. In County Tyrone, Northern Ireland, quilts were made with tops of red flannel two yards wide, bought locally and known as 'Swanskin'. The backing was usually of a coarse cotton or, more often, linen.[10]

Although cotton was imported to England as early as the fifteenth century the 'fill' of these quilts was commonly wool. When in the eighteenth century 'India quilts' became fashionable cotton was used for this purpose in some regions, notably near to manufacturing and importing centres like Durham, Northumberland, Yorkshire and Lancashire. In general wool and linen continued to be used in those regions where it was plentiful as in Ireland, the Isle of Man, South Wales, Westmorland and Cumberland.

Few examples of the bed-rug survive in America but I know of no British examples, although they must have once been common. In 1630 Governor John Winthrop of Massachusetts wrote to his son in England asking him 'to bring a store of Coarse Ruggs, both to use and to sell.'[11] The severe winters of North America made such articles very necessary but again and again references may be found to them in England. The *Dictionarium Brittanicum: Complete Universal Etymological English Dictionary*, published in London in 1730, describes a 'rugg' as a shaggy coverlet for a bed. In fact they were similar to a type of hooked rug very popular in the late nineteenth century for floors.

Others   The samplers made by girls at a tender age have been mentioned as have the woolwork pictures produced by the not-so-tender sailors. Decorative commemorative pincushions are another craft that sailors and women have in common. The earliest examples are those made by women prior to the birth of a baby, and most date from the eighteenth century, when pins were very expensive. As such cushions absorb a surprising number of pins, these charming objects were only for the rich. These pincushions usually carry a short verse:

> Welcome sweet Babe
> Welcome to sight
> May Angels attend thee
> By Day and by Night.

1   Quoted by Edward H. Pinto in *Treen and other Wooden Bygones*, Bell, London, 1969, page 114.
2   Old village woman recorded by Gertrude Jekyll; Gertrude Jekyll and Sydney R. Jones, *Old English Household Life*, Batsford, London, 1939.
3   See E. H. Pinto (1 above) page 118.
4   William Howitt, *Rural Life of England*, 1840.
5   Peter F. Brooks, *Pearly Kings and Queens in Britain*, Barry Rose Publishers, Chichester, Sussex, 1975.
6   *English Printed Textiles*, Victoria and Albert Museum booklet, 1960.
7   Elizabeth Hake, *English Quilting, Old and New*, Batsford, London, 1937.
8   G. Scott-Thompson, *The Russells in Bloomsbury*, London, 1940, pages 273–4.
9   *Sussex Archaeological Collection*, vol. IX, 1857, 'English Quilting', page 6.
10 Averil Colby, *Quilting*, London, 1972, chapter 4.
11 Quoted by Carleton L. Stafford and Robert Bishop, *America's Quilts and Coverlets*, New York, 1972, page 17.

Above right: *A late 18th century coverlet made from appliqué India chintz on cotton. 54in x 72in.*
Below right: *Two pincushions made for the birth of a child, and another 'maternity' pincushion with the verse worked in pins.*

Craft Industries

Above left: *Decorated dish from North Staffordshire, c1675.*
Above right: *Lead-glazed earthenware plate, mid–18th century.*

Pottery

Pottery was once made in every corner of the British Isles. Gradually a few centres became dominant, among them London, Bristol, Liverpool, Derby and above all the 'Five

Left: *An early 20th century brilliant-cut pub mirror with the trade mark and name of the company front-painted.*

Towns' in Staffordshire. Here we are concerned only with the earlier production of these centres and the work of the country potter that was made concurrently.

Ceramics are made from various clays fired at many temperatures. Porcelain is technically the most sophisticated. Pottery, or earthenware, may require only fairly rudimentary skills and equipment, and is thus a concern of this book. Stoneware is earthenware fired at a much higher temperature. The latter is frequently finished with salt glaze produced by throwing common salt into the kiln.

Most village pottery before the nineteenth century was of the simplest utilitarian kind except for certain decorative pieces used at festivals or at certain crucial times of the farming year. Coopered costrels were used to take cider into the fields at harvest time in many parts of England; in Sussex and Dorset and neighbouring counties pottery costrels of a decorative shape were common. Humour too

had its place in such examples as the 'Sussex pig', which had a body that provided a jug with a detachable head for a mug. These products of the Sussex potters were paralleled in Nottingham where stoneware 'bear mugs' were made in considerable numbers.

Sgraffito was a method of decorating pottery whereby the vessel was first covered with slip; once this was dry, designs could simply be scratched on, exposing the colour of the clay beneath. This method was particularly popular with

Top: *A jug in the form of an owl; the head comes off and serves as a mug; a 'cat' vase or jug, late 17th – early 18th century; Two-tiered hen and chickens money box impressed 'CHARRITY': possibly from Nottingham, 9½in high.*
Above left: *Two typical Bideford jugs, glazed in pale yellow with scratched inscriptions.*
Above right: *A harvest jug with sgraffito decoration: the design on the neck suggests the work of John Philips Hoyle of Bideford. Dated 1883, 11in high.*

Top: *Two aspects of a fine harvest jug with stylised oak leaf sgraffito decoration made by E. B. Fishley of Fremington, and an ornament by the same maker in the form of a loving cup with a removable lid. Decorated in relief and stamped on the front of the base, 'G. Fishley, Fremington', c1850, 8in high.*

Above: *A collection of pottery money boxes: an onion-shaped box in pale yellow glaze inscribed, 'Bideford 1902' and decorated with a butterfly and a rose. 6in high; a Halifax*

box with slip-trailed initials and date, 'JA 1865'. 5in high; Donyatt box inscribed 'DR' and 'October 20–1831'. 5½in high; a Bideford onion-shaped box with simple flower decoration, the reverse inscribed 'Bank 1897'. 5½in high.

the seventeenth and eighteenth-century potters of North Devon. The craftsmen of Barnstaple and Bideford used the clays of the Fremington bed with a strong 'grog', that is, clay which has been fired and ground down, which performs the function of letting the gases out. Their *sgraffito* harvest jugs are decorated with subjects either pastoral or nautical, an inevitable result of their geographical location.

The Fishleys were important potters in this region into the twentieth century, but the eighteenth-century George Fishley was the finest potter of the family, judging by his signed wares. Others working in this area in the late eighteenth century were Joseph Rice and Joseph Hollamore. At the village of Donyatt and at the hamlet of Crock Street, both near Ilminster, the *sgraffito* technique was also employed. The character of this south Somerset work is quite different from that produced by its North Devon neighbour. The Donyatt designs are much sparser, more angular, and indeed more scratchy, but in both these areas a yellow glaze flecked with green was used, derived from lead with copper impurities. At Donyatt the glaze was a deeper yellow, which influenced the colour of the white slip and the red ground more drastically but no less attractively than at Barnstaple. These potteries had been active before, but the last quarter of the seventeenth century was the time when their finest and most original work appeared. *Sgraffito* was also used as a means of decorating stoneware vessels made in Nottingham from about 1700 to 1830.

Slip (usually white) was one of the earliest ways of decorating a variety of items made of pottery (usually red or buff). There were many ways in which this slip or clay slurry could be applied. The surface of the host object

Below: Two-handled frog mug from Howcans pottery, Halifax, decorated with slip-trailed initials 'LL' and date '1889', 5½in high. Right: Puzzle jug with slip-trailed decoration and the name 'A. Kershaw 1860'. Halifax, 7½in high.

could be stamped with carved wood designs, as were medieval floor tiles and certain post-medieval work found in Sussex. (There is a good collection of this Sussex ware in Hastings Museum.)[1] The slip could then simply be poured into the resulting cavity and the surplus struck off with a strickle. The results of this technique are comparable with inlay in woodwork.

Perhaps the best known method of applying slip is to 'trail' it. By this method and with the assistance of a feather a marbled effect can be easily produced. This technique reached a height of perfection in Staffordshire in the last quarter of the seventeenth century with the work associated with the name Toft. The foremost of these was Thomas Toft; the names of other members of the family, among them Ralph and James, are also recorded on surviving pieces. Other names include William Talor, Ralph Simpson and John Wright. All of this so-called 'toftware' uses a dark slip on a light body. In contrast the Wrotham potters in Kent, George Richardson, John Eaglestone and Thomas Ifield, employed a buff slip on a dark ground.

Inevitably the favourite surface for this work was the simplest—the large plate or charger. Sometimes the slip was

132

applied to produce an abstract pattern but more popular was the central figure subject surrounded by a pattern and sometimes an inscription and date.

The elegant households of the eighteenth and nineteenth centuries were furnished with mantelpiece ornaments of porcelain. The 'image toys' (as Thomas Whieldon called them)[3] of the humble pottery were the modest equivalent for cottage and farmhouse. In the nineteenth century these objects—statuettes, watch-stands and the minature castles and cottages used as pastille-burners—were slip-cast and mass produced, but in the eighteenth century they were generally modelled individually. One of the earliest of these potters was John Astbury (1688–1743). 'Astbury' type work was not decorated with different-coloured glazes or slips, but was constructed of different-coloured clays with a simple, virtually colourless, salt glaze. This technique was also used in the production of veined or 'agate' wares. It has the pleasing effect of limiting the palette; the range is in fact limited to earth colours and their variations caused by impurities. The so called 'pew groups' (which represent figures seated on a settle), made in the first half of the eighteenth century, were characteristic of this work. They have all the fluidity and unconcern of a figure made of pastry.

Thomas Whieldon (d. 1789) has given his name to a whole class of work distinguished by it coloured glazes. He and his followers made figures of a charm that to some extent was born of the speed at which they were made. Pastoral subjects such as shepherds and shepherdesses were

Below: A pew group in saltglaze stoneware, c1745.
Right: Toby jug made in the style of Ralph Wood.

most popular, but bull-baiting was a fine bloodthirsty subject that was not missed. Portraits are also to be found. A Whieldon plaque of Sarah Malcolm (who was executed for a triple murder in 1733), is based on Hogarth's portrait of her. This type of work was so lively that it was able to benefit from continental influence and in effect to rise in social status with the work of Ralph Wood the Elder (brother of the block-cutter Aaron) and his son, both of whom developed this idiom to a level where it was respectable in many households. Their strength was maintained by roots deep in this Staffordshire tradition, in the context of which their Toby Jugs* and miniature christening cradles must be seen.

These pottery figures are in general small in size. The Willet Collection at Brighton Museum, however, includes an exception—a painted terra-cotta figure a couple of feet high that was apparently once a shop sign.

Tin glaze to decorate pottery was used at an early date by the delftware potters in England:

*Toby, like Punch, was an Italian importation, the mid-eighteenth century song 'The Brown Jug' being a loose translation by Francis Fawkes, published in 1761, of some verses in Latin by the Italian Geronomo Amalteo (1507—1574). (Article by Richard Aldington, *Times Literary Supplement*, 8 March 1923).

Pottery cradle: the red body has applied finial knobs and birds in white clay and a rich honey lead glaze. Possibly from Woodman House Pottery, Halifax. Mid–19th century.

About the Year 1567 *Jasper Andries* and *Jacob Janson* Potters, came away from *Antwerp*, to avoid the Persecution there, and settled themselves in *Norwich;* where they followed their Trade, making Gally Paving Tiles, and Vessels for Apothecaries and others very artificially. *Anno* 1570 they removed to *London* with the Testimonial of *Isbrand Balckius* and Minister; and the Elders and Deacons of that Church.[1]

Thus it was that the maiolica of Italy and Spain was introduced to England via the Low Countries. The earliest dated piece (in the Museum of London) with an inscription in English ('The Rose is Red The Leaves Are Grene God Save Elizabeth Ovr Queene . . . 1600') has an italianate appearance. Later Lambeth wares were of blue and white, a fashion caused by the flood of so-called Nankin porcelain from China. By the middle of the seventeenth century a distinctly English quality emerges and, in the second half of the century and throughout the eighteenth century, is generally pronounced. It is however often difficult to determine the origin of such work: London (Lambeth), Bristol, Wincanton or Liverpool. Among these wares there are some dashing pieces of folk art but many of the products of these towns were very sophisticated, and some even have a *chinoiserie* character.

Glass

Glass, like pottery, was once made in several parts of the British Isles but gradually a few places, for example Waterford and Bristol, became dominant. The Nailsea Glassworks were founded at Bristol in 1788, although the city had long been a centre of the industry exporting glass and even glassworkers to America. The Nailsea factory which closed in 1873 is important not only for the work that it actually produced but because it has given its name to a class of work that was also made by other establishments. Like most early glassworks these factories were primarily concerned with producing, for instance, window glass, which for some was still a luxury and regarded as such by government taxation. In their spare time the glassworkers used up left-over glass to make all manner of fanciful objects: pipes that were not to be smoked; and bells and post horns not destined for use but which nevertheless did produce notes. Strangest of all were the glass 'walking-sticks' made to hang in the house to absorb all diseases, and the 'witch-balls' of coloured blown glass which were hung in cottages as a protection against witchcraft.[2] A description of a cottage interior with such a walking-stick occurs in *John Ashby of Tysoe* by his daughter, M. K. Ashby:

> On the mantle-piece were china figures of old-fashioned policemen, pale blue-and-white, and small lions with

Nailsea glass pipe decorated in pink, white and blue. Early 19th century.

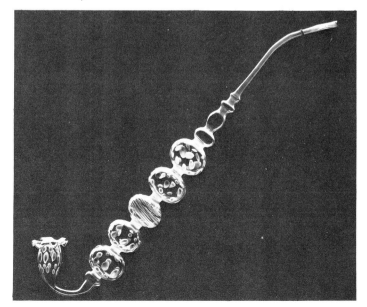

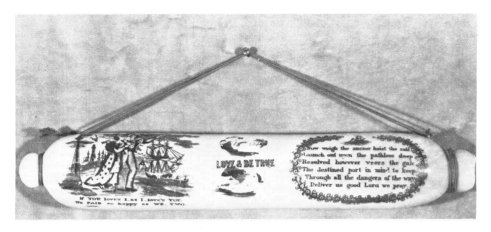

Above: *Two spun glass ship 'friggers' on a sea of spun glass.*
Above right: *Glass rolling pin with a sailor and his sweetheart, 'Love & Be True'. These were also used as salt containers.* Right: *Nautical glass rolling pin with the message 'Love and Live Happy'.*

crinkled manes. On the wall above were hung long hollow glass walking-sticks, twisted like barley sugar, one of them filled with tiny coloured balls like a confectioner's hundred and thousands.[3]

Even Friendly Society poleheads were sometimes made of glass in districts where the industry was active. 'Nailsea' spun glass was used to make all manner of fairings but birds, flowers and model ships were particularly popular.

Love tokens make their appearance in this material; ominously, the best known are rolling-pins. These are found widely distributed around the country and were presumably made in many places. They are painted and decorated with inscriptions bearing protestations of love, and are usually associated with sailors and their sweethearts:

If you loves I as I loves you
No pair so happy as we two.

The public house of the late nineteenth century was a reflection of the social stratification of England at that time. Unfortunately very few public house interiors have survived the attentions of interior decorators employed by the brewers. The physical barriers of mahogany and glass that

once divided class from class have been swept away. The cubicles created by these barriers—the public bar, the private bar, the snug, etc. also gave privacy to those who ignored the Temperance Movement, and the brilliant cut mirror-glass (which was sometimes front painted) gave a sense of space, without revealing too clearly the faces of the drinkers. Mirror-glass of this type was also used for photograph frames, and panels of it appear on fairground architecture.

Metal and Stone

Metal, especially steel, was a scarce commodity until the nineteenth century. For this reason carpenters when travelling took with them only the 'iron' of a plane, making up a 'stock' on arrival at the next job. Eighteenth-century sale catalogues and architectural books confirm the relative expense of metal. Nevertheless numerous objects survive that testify to the love with which this scarce commodity was handled. Some objects of brass, such as West Country poleheads, were mass produced, perhaps by 'Mr *Champion's* copper-works about three miles from Bristol'. The company specialised in making 'a vast number of awkward looking pans and dishes for the negroes, on the coast of Guinea.'[1] Some poleheads were individually made of tin (or even wood), painted and decorated. The earliest surviv-

Left: *Cast iron fireback probably depicting Christ at the well with the woman of Samaria.*
Above: *Stone lion from Freshford, near Bath, now sited over a house door, but once the local inn sign.*

ɪng specimens appear to date from the mid-eighteenth century, though most are of the nineteenth century.

Smiths, both black and white, have in their respective metals produced many objects of beauty as have the founders of brass, bronze and iron with, for example, horse-brasses and firebacks. Such cast objects were produced in numbers, if not mass produced. The smaller households could not afford firebacks; the backs to inglenook fires in cottage and farmhouse were often provided by non-structural brick nogging that could easily be replaced as it was gradually eaten away by the action of the fire.

Stone and marble are often referred to as if the words are synonymous but marble is a geologically distinct substance and has always been accepted as such by craftsmen who use different tools for it. As stone and marble are infinitely easier to carve than wood, it is remarkable that for the most part the 'folk' carver chose to work in wood, whereas the 'academic' sculptor of the nineteenth century seldom worked in this material. Even Gunnis in his *Dictionary of British Sculptors* and Margaret Whinney in her *Sculpture in Britain 1530–1830* speak of the 'extreme virtuosity' of Grinling Gibbons as wood-carver, but do not illustrate anything but his marble work. Occasionally in the districts of Britain where the stone was of exceptional quality examples of 'folk' sculpture in stone may be found —an occasional pub sign in the Bath area, for example, where the stone masons supplied not only their own locality

but the country at large. Such examples however are extremely rare. Much more common are the tombstones with which nearly every parish church in Britain (with the possible exception of Wales) is well endowed. Such church-yard monuments were rare in the seventeenth century, though the aristocracy and gentry exhibited the mortality of their progenitors in marble monuments of astounding magnificence within the church.

> Can storied urn or animated bust
> Back to it's mansion call the fleeting breath?[5]

With a more numerous and rising middle class in the eighteenth century, the churchyard of Gray's Elegy emerged, 'With uncouth rhymes and shapeless sculpture decked', and regional schools[6] of non-academic sculptors began to prosper. In the seventeenth century and before, stone was the common material—and it was not solely used to mark the graves of common people. Celia Fiennes in her *Journeys* (1697) observes that at Aitchison Bank on the Scottish side of the border with England, 'the Church-yard is full of grave stones pretty large with coats of armes and some had a coronet on the escutcheons cut in the stone . . .' Later this work falls into two main categories based on the materials used; on the one hand stone, slate and granite (sometimes employed in Cornwall) and on the other, marble, which was reserved for the high-class monuments inside the church. The 'local man' was sometimes entrusted with the fixing or repair of one of these marble monuments by one of 'our eminent artists', most of whom lived in the capital. J. T. Smith has some harsh things to say about these worthy craftsmen who, although famliar with their local materials, may not have had much experience of working in marble:

> —a fellow . . . with all the kindred and impenetrable hardness of his own granite, as soon as he is admitted into your presence, puts his mallet-hand to his side in

Above: *Elaborate engraved metal memorial plaque from the 17th century.* Right: *Hannah Twynnoy's tombstone from Malmesbury, Wiltshire.*

readiness to pull out his two-foot rule, which he is always sure to open at a right-angle, before he answers or even hears the question; and then, immediately after rubbing the back of his right ear, and most accurately measuring the fractured parts, hits upon a plan of cutting out the mutilations, by taking about *three inches* from the arm of the statue.[7]

Slate was extensively used in those districts, such as Cornwall and the Midlands, where the material is found. Because of the stratified structure of slate and also its hardness (though it can be easily split) the incised line can assume an almost calligraphic virtuosity of precision not only for lettering but also for decorative borders. Only with Westmoreland Green slate do the iron pyrites interrupt the flow of the chisel, a sacrifice that is readily made for the advantages of its colour.

Stone, like slate, can be easily incised, thought not with such knife-like arrises. The real virtue of stone is the freedom that it grants the skilful carver in the expression of form.

The quality of lettering on many headstones, footstones and ledgers is of a very high order. Not until the mid-nineteenth century is the effect of the printing press noticeable, with a resulting stiffness of line, formality of spelling and spaciousness of design—even the 'printer's rule' makes its appearance in these late works. Regrettably it was only in the nineteenth century that monumental masons began to sign their works regularly, and the authorship of most of the earlier fine examples is thus unknown to us.

1 Stow's *Survey of the Cities of London and Westminster and the Borough of Southwark*, quoted by Bernard Rackham and Herbert Read, *English Pottery*, New York, 1924.
2 George S. and Helen McKearin, *American Glass*, New York, 15th printing, 1963, page 179.
3 *Country Life*, 26 April 1962, 'Pottery Toys of the Image Maker' by Bea Howe.
4 Thomas Corbett, *A Six Week Tour through the Southern Counties of England and Wales*, 1768.
5 Thomas Gray, *An Elegy on a Country Churchyard*.
6 *Architectural Review*, November 1939. 'Rude Forefathers' by Innes Hart describes a school of carving in East Sussex, West Kent and part of Surrey.
7 J. T. Smith, *Nollekens and his Times*, 1919 ed., page 233.

Further Reading

Braithwaite, David *Fairground Architecture* London, 1968

Disher, M. Wilson *Fairs, Circuses & Music Halls* London, 1941

Dexter, T. F. G. *The Pagan Origin of Fairs* London, 1930

Fay, Arthur *Bioscope Shows and their Engines* London, 1966

Fletcher, Geoffrey S. *Popular Art in England* London, 1962

Haslemere Educational Museum *Guide to Peasant Arts* 1953

Heal, Sir Ambrose *London Tradesmen's Cards of the 18th century* London, 1925

Heal, Sir Ambrose *Signboards of Old London Shops* London, 1947

Jones, Barbara *The Unsophisticated Arts* London, 1951

Lambert, Margaret and Marx, Enid *English Popular Art* London, 1951

Larwood, Jacob and Hotten *History of Signboards* London, 1866

McKechnie, Samuel *Popular Entertainment through the Ages* London, 1931

Pinto, E. H. *Wooden Bygones of Smoking and Snuff Taking* London, 1961

Pinto, E. H. *Treen* London, 1970

Richardson, Sir Albert E. *The English Inn Past and Present* London, 1925

Richardson, Sir Albert E. *The Old Inns of England* London, 1934

Walford, C. *Fairs Past and Present* London, 1883

MAGAZINES

Lambert, Margaret and Marx, Enid *English Primitive Painting* New York, 'Antiques', May 1950

Little, Nina Fletcher *Popular Art for the American Motorist in Britain* New York, 'Antiques', April 1960

Ayres, James E. *British Folk Art at Freshford Manor* New York, 'Antiques', June 1971

NEWSPAPERS

Gaunt, William *The Genius of the Innocent Eye* London, 'The Times', 17th October 1967

Letters to 'Country Life' about Shop Signs, etc., 7th April, 6th June, 16th November 1967

Lady Bangor *All the Art of the Fair* London, 'The Observer' Colour Supplement, 14th May 1972

Hillier, Bevis *How it Pays to be Naïve* London, 'The Times', 20th October 1973

Emerson, Sally *Mrs Green and the World inside a Doll's House* London, 'The Times', 24th October 1973

Acknowledgments

Photographers' names appear in brackets

Colour

Albany Steam Museum, Newport, Isle of Wight (Angelo Hornak): facing page 49.
Lady Bangor's Fairground Collection, Wookey Hole, Somerset: facing page 48.
Blaise Castle Museum, Bristol: facing pages 40 and 65.
Cambridge Folk Museum (Angelo Hornak): facing page 32.
Angelo Hornak Collection: facing page 129.
Judkyn/Pratt Collection: facing pages 16, 17, 32, 33; between pages 40 and 41; facing pages 65, 80, 81, 96, 97, 104, 105, 112, 113 and 128.
Collection Mr and Mrs A. Kalman: facing page 64; between pages 104 and 105.
Museum of English Rural Life, University of Reading: facing page 64,
Roman Baths Museum, Bath: facing page 33.
Waterways Museum, Stoke Bruerne (Angelo Hornak): facing pages 64 and 65.

Black and white

Illustrations, where more than one appears per page, are listed from left to right in descending rows.

James Austin: 32d, facing 41, 73.
Author's Collection: 8, 18b, 21a, 21b, 22, 28a, 100.
Lady Bangor's Fairground Collection, Wookey Hole, Somerset: 58b, 58c, 59a, 59b, 60b, 60c, 60d, 60e, 61a.
Collection C.A. Bell-Knight: 95b.
Bethnal Green Museum: 122b.
By permission of Birmingham Museum and Art Gallery: 58a, 69c, 75a, 118b, 121c.
Blaise Castle Museum, Bristol: 59b, 68, 84a, 96a, facing 97, 117a, 119.
Bord Fáilte: 123a.
Bristol City Museum: 42b.
British Library (Ray Gardner): 12a, 12b, 12c, 13, 14a, 72a, 116a.
British Museum, Crace Collection (John R. Freeman): 31, 54b, 55, 66, 72b.
Buckler's Hard Village and Maritime Museum, Hampshire: 74.
Cambridge Folk Museum (Angelo Hornak): 17, 30, 37c, 45a, 45b, 75e, 95a, facing 97, facing 128.
Castle Museum, York: 56c, 56d, 57a, 57b, 57d, 80b, 83a, 83b.
Colchester and Essex Museum: 106b, 107, 108.

By kind permission of Messrs. Coutts & Co.: 120.
Crown Copyright, National Monuments Record: 105a, 105b.
Crown Copyright, Victoria & Albert Museum: 18a, 28b, 41, 49a, 96c, facing 97, 121a, 122a, 126b, 127c, 134b.
Dorchester Museum: 46.
Mary Evans Picture Library: 23b, 23c, 48b, 103a.
Fitzwilliam Museum, Cambridge: 129a, 129b, 130a, 130b, 133a.
Guildhall Library, City of London: 53, 60a, 67a, 67b.
By kind permission of Ind Coope (Ian Cameron): 106a.
Judkyn/Pratt Collection: 7, 10, 15a, 34a, 36c, 51a, 56b, 75c, 79a, 79b, 84b, 84c, 85, 86a, 86b, 87a, 87b, 88b, 89a, 89b, 90b, 90c, 90d, 92b, 92c, 92d, 92e, 93, 94a, 94b, 98a, 99a, 101, 102a, 103b, 121b, 126c.
Collection Mr and Mrs A. Kalman: 47a, 47b.
A.F. Kersting: 26.
Collection Reg Lloyd: 130b, 130d, 130e, 131a, 131b, 131c, 131d, 132a, 132b, 134a.
The Mansell Collection: 23d, 62a, 70, 71, 75d, 125b.
Museum of English Rural Life, University of Reading: 9b, 9c, 9d, 63, 64a, 64b, 80a, 102b, 113a, 113b, 114a, 116b, 118a, 123b, 124a, 125a, 135a, 135b, 136a, 137b.
Museum of English Rural Life, Brotherton Collection: 51b, 51c. Mrs M. Fuller: 133b. C.D. Hartley: 51d. Luton Museum: 89c, 114b, 124c. Molesworthy Museum, Devon: 135c. C.J.G. Short: 50. J. Tarlton: 9a. Welsh Folk Museum: 118d. Miss Wright: 117b, facing 128, 137a.
National Maritime Museum; Michael Holford Library: 75b.
National Museum of Wales; Welsh Folk Museum: 67c, 90a, 117c, 126a, 127a, 127b.
Norfolk Museums Service; Strangers' Hall Museum: 32a, 33, 35, 36a, 36b, 38b, 39a, facing 40, 42a, 44.
Oxford Public Library: 54a, 61b, 62b.
Trustees of the Pierpont Morgan Library: 43.
Collection Mrs Polly Rogers: 91, 92a.
Popperfoto: 75f.
The Royal Academy of Arts: 15b.
Somerset County Museum: 124b.
Sotheby & Co.: 29c, 98b.
The Tate Gallery, London: 29a.
Town Docks Museum, Kingston upon Hull Council: 96a, 69b, 76a, 76b, 77a, 77b, 77c, 77d.
Tunbridge Wells Museum, Kent: 82, 85, 87c, 87d, 88a, 88c.
By kind permission of the Warden, Urchfont Manor: 99a.
Victoria & Albert Museum (A.C. Cooper): 14b, 23a, 25a, 81, 94c, 111.
Weston Gallery, Norwich: 56a.
The Wills Collection of Tobacco Antiquities, Bristol: 38a, 38c.

Index